The Military Millionaire

THE MILITARY MILLIONAIRE

A Financial Lifestyle Guide for
Service Members and Their Families

by Ken Heaney
Lieutenant Colonel Army Retired

Edited by
Robin Miller

Order this book online at www.trafford.com
or email orders@trafford.com

Most Trafford titles are also available at major online book retailers.

Lieutenant Colonel, U.S. Army Retired and Registered Representative,
National Planning Corp.

Printed in the United States of America.

ISBN: 978-1-4269-4343-0 (sc)
ISBN: 978-1-4269-4344-7 (hc)
ISBN: 978-1-4269-4345-4 (e)

Library of Congress Control Number: 2010913504

*Our mission is to efficiently provide the world's finest, most comprehensive book publishing
service, enabling every author to experience success. To find out how to publish your
book, your way, and have it available worldwide, visit us online at www.trafford.com*

Trafford rev. 10/18/2010

 www.trafford.com

North America & international
toll-free: 1 888 232 4444 (USA & Canada)
phone: 250 383 6864 ♦ fax: 812 355 4082

For Mom and Dad

Acknowledgements

Thanks to Robin Miller for his editorial work. He's a real friend of the military. Thanks to Kelly Almon for her work with the graphics. Finally, thanks to Andy Downs for keeping me compliant. He knows what I mean.

Contents

INTRODUCTION

I'm thoroughly enjoying military retirement. I'm also enjoying representing my clients and serving as an investment professional. So why go through the trials of writing an investment guide for the military? Here's why:

I was at a birthday party near Philadelphia, Pennsylvania. My cousin had turned 60 and her husband, Charlie, threw a surprise party for her complete with an open bar serving free beer and wine. The bartender was busy pouring glasses of White Zinfandel and mugs of Yuengling Ale from the tap. He looked up at me and asked "wine or beer buddy?" I always try to engage strangers in conversation. I guess the habit comes for hanging out on the tarmack at Green Ramp with time to kill waiting to load the aircraft for an airborne operation. I'd pass the time by striking up a conversation with anyone willing to talk. So I responded to the bartender "Do I look like the beer or wine type?" "Neither really," he said. I asked "Do you have any scotch under the bar?" "Let's see," he said. "Well, here's a bottle of Johnie Walker Red." That will do." I flipped a 20 dollar bill on the bar as a gratuity and said "I don't drink much so this should cover you for the night." The bartender took the twenty, looked it over, then looked me over and asked, "Hey, are you in the mafia?" With a dead pan face, I narrowed my eyes, leaned over the bar and in my best South Philly accent answered, "forget about it and don't ask questions." Outside, I was completely stoic. Inside, I was ready to double over and crack up. That's what I get for wearing my double breasted "GoodFellas" suit to an Italian restaurant in Philadelphia and over tipping the bartender. Then my brother joined me at the bar: slicked back hair, opened collar and gold chain around his neck. For the rest of the night, the bartender and wait staff could not do enough to keep us happy.

So what does this incident have to do with writing THE MILITARY MILLIONAIRE? Only this: It was at this party that I bumped into another cousin of mine who is an executive at a major telecommunications company. I had not see him for a couple of years, but noticed he was sporting a yellow rubber bracelet. I asked what the bracelet was for and he said, "I support the troops." "Hey, that's great," I said. What do you do to support the troops? "What do you mean?" he asked. "I mean, what do you do to support the troops? Do you send them phone cards, or care packages or something like that?" "No, I just wear the bracelet," he said. I was disappointed and a little saddened. My cousin is a real stand up guy, loves America and is the son of a World War II veteran, but like so many well intentioned Americans, he probably didn't know *what to do* to support the troops except for wearing the bracelet. So many people I meet think that supporting the troops means wearing a bracelet or putting a bumper sticker on their car. For me, that is just not enough. So, besides the numerous care packages I send overseas, I want to do something a little more tangible for the troops. I decided to pull together some thoughts for you—our military members and families—with a goal of improving your financial future by presenting the opportunities available to you and improving your quality of life and wellbeing.

In addition to this book, I've also developed a free website: www.mymilitarymillionaire.com where military and family members can go for a single source of relevant financial and military benefit information and services that they can really use. Here you can obtain copies of THE MILITARY MILLIONAIRE, find useful financial calculators, information, seminars and links. You can also contact me directly through the website. I welcome your feedback and conversation. If there's something you'd like seeing posted on the website, send me a note and I'll do my best to add it. This is my way of saying "thanks for *your* sacrifice so *we* don't have to." One of the great things of becoming a military millionaire is that it becomes easier to give back to others as well as provide for your family.

Becoming a military millionaire doesn't require a big salary, corporate bonus checks or tremendous prowess in stock, commodity or real estate markets. It does require taking advantage of the generous resources the military offers, of using a systemic approach to investing in your future, and avoiding the pitfalls that people routinely fall in because they don't have a plan. I believe that wealth is obtainable to the military professional without sacrificing devotion to duty or family. It's simply a matter of loading up your financial rucksack with the goals, a plan, the right information and applying sound lifestyle habits that take advantage of what's available to you as a service member or family member and avoiding poor financial and lifestyle decisions. I'd like to give you the answers to the test in advance so you can get it right the first time. So come on and follow me!

Chapter One

Your Pay and Benefits

"Life just doesn't hand you things.
You have to get out there and make things happen."
Chef Emeril Lagasse

Nobody I know has enough money, no matter how much they have. As an investment professional I represent and talk with people all the time about money. I have yet to meet anyone, including myself, who has enough money. OK, I have enough money for me, but my wife insists that we're teetering on the brink of poverty and that I need to make more. Does that sound familiar? At least that's what she said while we were on the way to the granite boutique to pick out her new kitchen counter tops. It's an amazing phenomenon that nobody has enough money. Convicted "Ponzi Schemer" Bernie Madoff wasn't satisfied with stealing 60 billion dollars from his investors, so he stole more. Hopefully, we all know when we've had enough to eat, or enough to drink. Most people know when they have had enough sleep and get up out of bed. But for some reason people never seem to be satisfied with their income. And if you're dissatisfied with you're income now that your working full time with a full time income, then you'll really hate retirement when your income may be truly limited, or even worse, you may feel in a you won't really be able to retire at all.

My niece, who is a client, has recently entered the job market earns in a month what I made in a year as an Army lieutenant. But she doesn't think she makes enough. I have another client who made in bonuses, not counting her salary, more than I made as an Army lieutenant colonel. She too thinks she doesn't make enough income as well. She and her husband have a portfolio exceeding 2 million dollars, yet they express concern over their financial future.

Personally, I feel fortunate that I'm in a position to influence my income. Simply put, the more I work at my investment practice the more I'm capable in bringing home. But with that incentive of greater pay for more work comes a price. The price of sacrificing the other things I could be doing rather than working. Such things might include participating in my son's Boy Scout program, or coaching the local high school football team or taking my mom on a trip or something as simple as cooking meals. I do all of these because I've been able to avoid the illusion that "with just a little bit more income, all my financial needs and wants would be met." This idea of making more money to solve all one's problems is a mirage. The closer you get to the mirage the further away you're getting from the ones and things that really matter. When I was attending Army Ranger School in the winter of 1984, it was common for the starving and exhausted Ranger students to see things that weren't there. On one patrol I kept stooping to pick up what I thought were cookies on the trail. I saw a Ranger student try to put imaginary coins into a tree thinking it was a Coke machine. I even saw a Ranger student try to order a pizza on the squad radio. We were all experiencing false realities of what was really occurring. Sure, money can solve some problems, but there are many better and easier approaches to problem solving than working oneself into an early grave in order to "make enough money." A very wise man once said that *true wealth means needing nothing.* In my own life, tempering my needs makes me feel wealthy. People tell me it shows on my face. Once a stranger came up to me at an airport and said to me "You look like you're worth a million bucks!" I may look like a million, but I fly coach.

Still have doubts about needing more income? Talk to senior citizens who have earned prosperity in life. They typically talk about life in terms of achievements and experiences rather than possessions. In the end of life, we all want to be surrounded by family and friends. Nobody wants to be surrounded only by things. In my own life I've accumulated a lot of stuff. I'd like to spend the second half of my life divesting myself the clutter and focusing on building relationships and experiences. Does this sound like you too?

Besides the perception of low pay, the most difficult elements of a military career are demands of duty. There's no getting around it. As a career, the military is an exceptionally demanding journey. But having been retired from the military for more than 6 years, I find that the business world can be just as demanding. I have about 250 investment clients, so I know many corporate types who work exhausting hours that are comparable to what we work in the military. Do yourself a favor and don't waste energy envying how easy other folks have it in civilian life. Do I have it easy now? Of course, I worked very hard during my military career to achieve my current lifestyle, and I'm just as busy as before. I have more things to do than I can possibly get done. Working hard was a key component of achieving my goals. The difference is that I'm driving events instead of events driving me. I don't think I would enjoy it as much had I not embarked on a military career before my second civilian career. The military career gives one the body of experience necessary to really enjoy life after the military.

One of the main differences between the military and the business world is that the military has a very defined compensation plan and pay schedule, while the business world often builds flexibility into what it pays its employees for recruitment and retainment. The recent political debate over the bonuses AIG paid its executives is a public example. As with my client who makes large bonuses, her compensation is flexible and dependent upon the revenue her team brings into the company. So it's not unusual that her bonuses exceed her base pay. However, in the military we have relative predictability with our pay and benefits. I'll show you steps to help you use that predictability to your advantage.

After the Military

When I retired in 2003 I weighed starting an investment practice against working for a corporate giant. I talked with friends in various industries and tried to learn the good, the bad and the ugly about each. My investment firm partner and 20 year friend, Bruce Brown, knew me very well and was exceedingly persuasive in getting me to join the investment firm.

We traveled to Dana Point, California, during one of the producer's conferences sponsored by our broker-dealer. We stayed at the St. Regis Hotel at Dana Point. I was impressed by the opulence of the place, a far cry from the low budget places I used to stay at while traveling with the military. On one temporary duty assignment (TDY), I sent a postcard to my parents from where I was quartered describing it to be "as creepy as the Bates' Motel from the movie *Psycho!*" My mom still has that postcard. On another TDY trip I was provided a rucksack full of MREs and slept just off the flight strip under a poncho liner at Charleston Air Force base until my mission was completed.

So here I was on the beautiful California beach with my friend Bruce talking about what I should do after retirement from the Army. He said if I joined the investment firm, I'd have costs associated with studying for and taking my licensing tests and expenses for maintaining my securities and insurance licenses, not to mention the cost of errors and admissions (read malpractice) insurance. I'd have office overhead expenses along with employee salaries and taxes to pay and no guarantee that anyone would be interested in signing with me as a client and therefore no guarantee of income. However, Bruce convinced me that being able to drive events in establishing my own investment practice would be gratifying. He also convinced me that the same qualities that served me so well in the military-- honesty, integrity and taking care of others-- would be the same qualities that would make me a successful investment professional. Best of all, for the first time in 20 years, I wouldn't have a place I'd have to be at or a boss to satisfy.

Bruce also convinced me that there would be no shortage of investors who would want to sign on with me in order to tap my 20 years of investment experience and reputation for hard work and dedication.

While interviewing with another company in Northern Virginia I took away a golden nugget that I pass on to others thinking about their future. I was interviewing with a former professional acquaintance from the Army who was recruiting me for his firm. I presume he was looking for someone close to the US Army Special Operations Command, because his company had not yet tapped that lucrative market. His company had a presence on Fort Bragg, but had not made its way across post to Special Ops. I had worked there on and off for a number of years so the company thought I might be the one to help them tap the Special Ops market.

After the usual discussion about what I could do and what contacts I had, the interviewer asked "Ken, I hear all the things you *can* do and I've known you long enough to know that you can get a lot done, but here's my question. What do you *want* to do?" That question made me rethink how I was approaching retirement. It really set me to thinking about what I might want to do. It also made me grateful for my financial decisions, military benefits and lifestyle choices that had put me in a position that allowed me to do what I *wanted* to do, rather than just doing a job I *could* do. How great would it be for you when you retire from the military to be able to pursue the second career that you *want* to do during retirement? Most don't think about how much they do in the military influences what they do after the military.

So, by the end of my discussions with Bruce Brown, Kenyon International, Bearing Point, IBM, and others. I decided to take a calculated risk and establish my own investment practice. This is one of the best decisions I've ever made--almost as good as my decision to stay military until retirement eligibility. Even with the severe economic and market downturn over the last couple of years, I can't imagine enjoying any profession any more than I do as an investment professional—except for a military career.

In just a few short years after that one difficult decision, I now manage my own investment practice and have a great group of clients who I consider friends first. Sometimes I still can't believe how fortunate I am to have the opportunity to share my many years of investment experience with so many clients everyday. I'm grateful to be doing what I want to do most. Even today, with the economy at its worst in decades, I'm in a position to help my loyal clients navigate through a very difficult investment climate.

Financial Advantages of a Military Career

For a Money Section article, *USA TODAY* asked me "What is the best financial move you've ever made?" I responded that it was staying military. I still believe that, besides the intrinsic rewards associated with selfless service, the military pension plan is one of the best out there. Never underestimate the value of a fully funded pension plan. If I live to the average of my life expectancy of my family, I will likely make double in retirement pay what I made in active duty. That's amazing. Even more amazing is that only a small minority of Americans are covered by a fully funded pension plan. Such a pension is a powerful means to financial security and personal well-being.

Although I was anxious to start my investment practice, it took more than desire to get it off the ground. It was critical to have a solid portfolio and savings along with the current income and benefits that my military retirement provides. These assets gave me the time and space I needed to get my investment services practice up and running. Because of military retirement I didn't need to worry about current income, health insurance, dental insurance, life insurance or survivor benefits. All of these wonderful benefits are currently available with the military pension.

As for you, you're on the right track by continuing you military career. I know it's tough. Deployments, sea duty, the wars in Iraq and Afghanistan require even more sacrifice from you and your family than it is fair to ask of anyone. You do it with style, finesse, patriotism and all the character that makes America so great. But, you may be tempted to leave the military before retirement eligibility in order to pursue another way of life. But I hope to convince you that military service can be consistent with a rewarding career both professionally and financially. **If you're thinking about leaving the service, think twice. This guide will provide more facts on why a military career and retirement can be very rewarding and a great way to launch into a second career after retirement.**

When I talk with service members, there seems to be a prevailing sentiment that the compensation for military service is inadequate,—that somehow one is losing financial ground by staying military. I hear it all the time, almost as much as well intentioned folks who wear yellow bracelets to support the troops, but do little else to actually support them. My own nephew left the Navy after about 8 years of service to go to school. I tried but failed to convince him to hang in there. Also, my lawn service guy lamented, "Ken, it hit me this week that had I stayed in the Army, I'd be able to retire about now. If I had made it to retirement, I could be running my lawn service business and not worrying about the economy nearly as much." I hear similar regrets over and over again from those who bailed out. My own father who left the Army as a Corporal and went on to have a successful 40 plus year career with Sun Oil Company often talked about missing out by not staying in the Army. One the other hand, I have never, ever met a military retiree who wished he had cut his or her military career short.

I can understand when soldiers and Marines tell me they are exhausted from the deployment cycles associated with the wars in Iraq and Afghanistan. Most non-military Americans just can't appreciate how demanding these deployments are on the military and their families. They often shrug it off saying "Well, that's what they signed up for." These folks will never understand what it takes to serve. I empathize with service members who opt out early, rather than continually putting themselves in harm's way. **But if you're thinking of leaving before retirement due to low pay, I hope to convince you otherwise.**

During my own military career I've been able to amass a portfolio that will allow me to own multiple homes, give to charities, send my son to any college he can get accepted to and even pay my wife's monthly credit card bill. I'm sometimes amazed at how far we've come financially. **And we did it by staying military.** *You can too!*

Living Out of My Car

I can understand how you may feel that financial independence is a mirage and that seeking more pay in the civilian sector is what's real. However, you can with some knowledge and a little discipline can achieve financial independence and personal well-being. When I joined the Army as a second lieutenant in 1983 I was deeply in debt with student loans and consumer debt. I had paid for much of my college myself and did not even receive an ROTC scholarship (foolishly). Unfortunately, I didn't get paid until a month or so after reporting to Fort Benning, Georgia, due to an uncaring or unresponsive pay system. I had less than $200 in my pocket which was not enough to make a deposit on an apartment. To make matters worse, there was a waiting list to get into post bachelor officers quarters (BOQ) so I slept in my car and on the floor of a friend's BOQ room until I could get into my own room, on credit I might add. So I started my military and financial journey deeply in debt and ended it with more assets that I will likely spend in my lifetime.

When interviewed for an article for *USA TODAY*, the original article talked about how I went from living in my car as a second lieutenant to being a wealthy major. I asked *USA TODAY* to cut out that part of the article. They also left out the part about me being so poor while attending University of Delaware that I often had to choose between eating and putting gas in my car to get to work. I can recall being out with friends and pretending I was not hungry because I could not afford the price of a hamburger. No kidding, this was a really tough time for me. I often had to choose between food for my stomach and fuel for my car. For me the college experience was tougher than Ranger School. The reason is that at Ranger School, we all suffered alike. At college, I was on my own, except for the kindness of family and friends who helped me through the toughest times. I never even considered quitting Ranger School, but I wanted to quit college almost everyday. I confided this to family, friends and some clergy who were very supportive. They know who they are and I will always appreciate it. But, I came from a home with a strong work ethic. My parents and siblings were all hard workers and I felt like I was slacking off by going to college instead of going to work full time. Later, that work ethic I inherited would pay off during my career.

If I can attain some measure of financial independence without losing my integrity or American spirit, so can you. I've been blessed with no special abilities, just the desire to do better. *You can do it, so let's get started!*

The first step of the Military Millionaire is to accept the premise that a military salary is enough. Sure, more money would be great, but you can make enough for many circumstances. Besides making enough now, you can count on a cost of living raise every year. Some years it is a little, some years it is a lot. It doesn't always work that way in the civilian world. Furthermore, a significant portion of your salary is not taxed. Even better, if you're deployed to a combat zone your income may be tax free. Do you know how much more money is in your pocket due to the combat zone tax exclusion? For us working in the corporate world it can be stunning how deeply the government can reach into our pockets for taxes.

We often underestimate the value of tax free money. My former military clients are universally shocked when they realize their tax bill after retirement. While we're working on retirement strategies I often tell them that their primary issue after retirement will be taxation, especially when and embarking on a second career. Income *will not* be their primary concern. Without exception this has been true. Can you believe that in higher income brackets pay as much as 35 cents in federal tax on every dollar earned in addition to state and local taxes? There's talk among politicians to tax so-called excess wages at nearly 100 percent. Talk about getting a W-2 wedgie that will make your eyes water! So enjoy your reduced taxation requirements while you're on active duty because you'll likely be paying some heavy duty taxes when you retire and embark on a second career.

Generals and Admirals for Peanuts

Most of us have a pretty good understanding of our military base pay, which is based on pay grade and years of service. For instance on the 2009 pay chart, the lowest basic pay for an enlisted person (E-1) with less than 2 years of service is **$1347** per month. At the top end of the pay chart, the highest pay for a 4 star flag officer (O-10) is **$17,383**. However, the Chairman of the Joint Chiefs of Staff makes a little over **$18,600** per month base pay. So, the senior leaders of the military make about 13 times that of the newest recruits. At first thought, that may seem unbalanced or unfair, but I guarantee that if one looks at many major corporations, the senior leaders are making more than **$14,560** a month, which is generally 13 times the minimum wage of their entry employees. In fact, it would not be hard to find corporate CEOs who are making more than $14,560 a day! *Yes, a day!* One member of the Obama administration is reported to have made $100,000 a day in consultation fees (Source: April 26, 2009 *Fox News Sunday*) before joining the administration. That's $100,000 per day! If an entry level employee at that firm made $7.50 per hour, which would be a daily wage of $60.00. The member of the Obama administration previously making $100,000 a day theoretically made more than 1600 times what the entry-level person might have made compared to the 13 times salary that a 4 star general or admiral makes over a private or E-1. So, the senior leaders of the military have duties and responsibilities commensurate with our corporate leaders, but they do it on the cheap. We are fortunate to have leaders like General Petraeus and General McChrystal as well as other generals and admirals who take on such tremendous responsibility they do and for relative peanuts. Clearly our senior military leaders don't do it for the money. They deserve our respect.

The military pay chart figured into my decision to retire from the military years ago. Pay raises associated with moving up the ladder of military rank were not enough to keep me in, even though at the time of my decision to retire, I was competitive for promotion and at the top of my branch year group.

Similarly, most service members seem to have a good understanding of the various proficiency and incentive pays, such as Aviation, Airborne, Sea, Dive, Submariner, Professional, Drill Pay and the rest. I was talking with a retired Lieutenant General, who led the 82D Airborne Division during the Panama Invasion, Operation Just Cause. He told me with a smile that part of his decision to go Airborne was for the extra $50 per month in jump pay. I spent about 15 years on jump status myself and there's not enough money in the military pay system to compensate me for the bumps I've taken while parachuting. On the other hand, it was a blast to do and I'd do again and for free if there were not jump pay.

Not all of us get to be the Commander of an Army or Marine Division, Naval Fleet or a numbered Air Force. In fact, hardly any of us ever rise to that level of responsibility or rank. However, I know noncommissioned officers who have made great financial decisions and have portfolios comparable with many general officers. I know because everyday I look at financial portfolios for a living. I retired as only a Lieutenant Colonel, rising to mid-level management in the military industrial complex, and would not trade my financial position with anyone I know regardless of their rank. By now you should be convinced that it's not how much you make, *but it's how you make use of what you make*!

Chapter Two

Getting Started with Goals

"The journey of a thousand miles starts with a single step."
Lao-Tzu (604BC-531BC)

My clients sometime try to guess to what I attribute my financial success. Some believe its uncanny market timing. Some think it's because I don't freely spend money. Some may even think it's been given to me. But none of these assertions is quite right. In fact, I don't believe in trying to time the market; rather, I believe in a systematic and life long approach to investing. I don't believe I'm particularly tight fisted with my income, and I have never inherited a dime. *The first step toward financial success is developing goals and a timeline to achieve those goals.*

Did you know you can set relevant and long term financial goals and build a financial strategy on just two pieces of paper? One piece is for your goals and the other is for your time line. I'll explain how to do this, just as I did. I also share this method of capturing goals and plans with my clients. It's a great tool for being able to visualize your financial future. If you're married or have children, it's important to share your goals with your family and get their input and buy in. In fact, it's a good idea to have them sign it.

Establish Your Goals

When I joined the Army I was in debt with college and car loans and credit cards. I volunteered for an assignment to the Republic of Korea, partly, because I knew the mission would be all consuming while affording me the opportunity to pay off my debts and come home from Korea with some savings. So my first goal was to get out of debt in my 1-year short tour. Not only did I accomplish my goal, but also my battalion commander insisted that I extend for an extra three months in Korea, which helped with my savings. However, I was anxious to get back to the States and my follow-on assignment at Fort Bragg with the 82D Airborne Division, so I was disappointed when my battalion commander insisted on my extension in Korea. I managed to accomplish my goal, but the goal was short sighted.

What the aspiring *MILITARY MILLIONAIRE* needs to do first is establish long term goals. Twenty years out is just about right for long term goals. In fact, it's useful to look at one's financial future in 20 year blocks of time. The first 20 years of life are usually dedicated to youthful pursuits, the second 20 years toward building a career, the third 20 years in pursuing a second career and fourth 20 years enjoying the fruits of the first 60 years. If I'm lucky enough to get a 5th 20 years, I hope I can enjoy it as much as my mother and her brother are doing. They really know how to enjoy life and make everyday count.

Regardless of how long we live, there's no mistaking that long term goal setting is the first step of a financial journey. So after finally returning from Korea and quickly realizing how much I enjoyed serving in the 82D Airborne Division and Fort Bragg, I established a long term goal to remain in the Army until retirement eligibility and then be financially secure enough to live off a military retirement after 20 years of service.

I believe the best way to set long term goals is to take the time to write them down as I have done for myself and my clients. First I started with a simply worded goal:

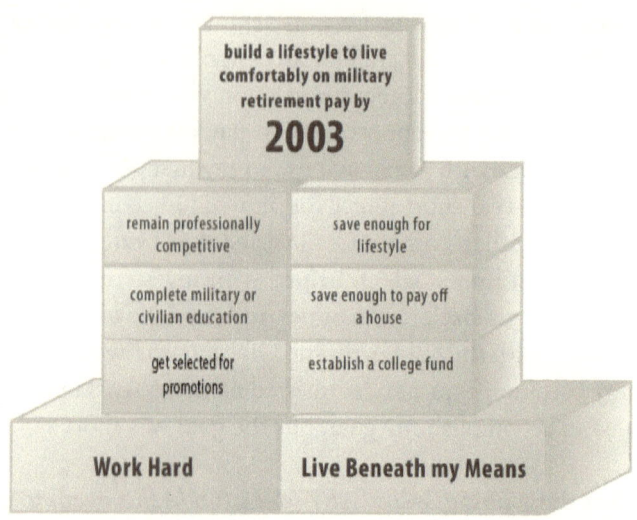

build a lifestyle to live comfortably on military retirement pay by

2003

remain professionally competitive	save enough for lifestyle
complete military or civilian education	save enough to pay off a house
get selected for promotions	establish a college fund

Work Hard **Live Beneath my Means**

Simply stated, my goal back in 1985 was to "Establish a lifestyle such that I could live comfortable on a military retirement by 2003." I didn't get all crazy about trying to define what living comfortably meant. I intuitively knew it meant being able to meet my obligations, enjoy some entertainment and travel and still be able to sleep at night without the worry of debt. Then I added the steps in descending order that would lead me to my goal from my current place in life. This is consistent with "military reverse planning." I found that my goal really had two implicit goals: first, become retirement eligible and second, build the portfolio necessary to augment a military retirement.

I didn't know that making it to military retirement would require me to survive the Army drawdown of the mid-1990s. In fact, my math suggests that less than half of my year group survived the Army drawdown to make it to major. I was fortunate to have mentors who helped me navigate that very difficult period of my career. Ironically, at the time of the Army draw down I was working on drawdown plans for the Army. I would have had to draft my own separation letter had I been selected for the "Reduction in Force (RIF)." Only in the military! I make mention of this because I believe a military drawdown may be in the future. The government is digging such a deficit hole that the military budget may be the most socially palatable place for budget cuts because Social Security, Medicare and Medicaid seem to be untouchable for budget cuts. Military budget cuts could touch nearly a million uniformed service members. However, Social Security, Medicare and Medicaid cuts could touch as many as 200 million Americans, which is politically a non-starter. Your financial readiness will be a key to sleeping soundly should the military be called upon to reduce its ranks as it did during my career. I hope I'm wrong that a RIF is inevitable, but there is no easy way for the Nation to reduce its budget deficit and debt.

So, with the guidance of my military mentors, officers, noncommissioned officers, and civil servants I learned that steps to remaining professionally competitive would require completion of civilian and military education and certain career enhancing jobs. I learned that the steps to getting these opportunities meant simply working hard, doing the right thing by commanders and soldiers and staying close to my mentors. And work hard I did, just as you are working hard at your military career.

In addition to the career component to my goal, I knew there was a financial component. To live comfortable on a military pension, I'd need to augment my retirement pay with some outside income. I figured that I could earn up to $300 per month of income of an investment of $50,000. If that sounds like a lot of interest, remember that 1985 was not long after the President Carter and early President Reagan years when interest rates were in double digits. We may be seeing a similar rise in interest rates in our future, again, fueled by our growing budget deficit. Also, I'd want to be in a position to pay off my house upon retirement which meant saving $55000 during my career. I also felt that I would not be comfortable if I did not have at least something put aside for education so I figured that $2,000 would be a good start. The educational savings wasn't originally intended for me but for my children. It may seem excessive, but I started saving for my son's education years before he was even born—even before I was married. Coincidentally, I talked with a friend my age who is still about $16,000 in debt for his daughter's college education. He remarked to me that his original plan involved his mother-in-law paying for her college education. That source of funding never materialized, so at a time when my friend should be enjoying the fruits of his previous 30 years of work, he's struggling to finish paying off college bills. When I encouraged him by saying that he was doing the right thing and he responded that he wished he had done the right thing 20 years ago and started a college fund for his daughter.

Finally, it became very obvious that to save for education, to pay off my house and to augment my military retirement, I'd need to have something left at the end of the month after paying bills. Simply put, I'd need to live beneath my means. Ultimately, that meant a standard of living one pay grade beneath my rank. When I was a captain, I lived on lieutenant pay and invested and saved the difference. As a major, I lived on captain pay and saved the rest. During the years that my wife worked outside the house, we worked at saving or investing all of her income.

So, to reach my goal to live a comfortable lifestyle on a military retirement by 2003, I would need to do two very basic tasks: First, work hard. Second, live beneath my means. What could be simpler? During my military career I was known for possessing a tremendous work ethic and driving a really crappy car. **Does working hard and living beneath your means have a place in your plan? I hope so.**

Since most of the officers I served with were much brighter and more talented than me, my edge was to out work them. For instance, when I became the Chief of Officer Management for the 82D Airborne Division, I worked everyday, approximately 15 hours per day, for 123 days straight before I took my first half day off. My first half day off was on Labor Day, 1989. I met my wife at the officer club for a late lunch and a swim. When we got home around 5PM there was this message on my home answering machine from my boss: "Ken, I called your office this afternoon and did not reach you. It's great that you can take off in the middle of a Monday. Call me when you get this." Ugh!

I kept the same work ethic for my entire military career, except for my year at Marine Corps Command and Staff College at Quantico, Virginia. I missed a lot of school that year because I had an Air Force team leader who was sympathetic to my geo-bachelor status. My family was in Maryland and I was living at Quantico, Virginia, about 90 miles away. Near the end of the school year the commandant of the school called me to his office to ask me how it could be that I missed so much of his esteemed school. After granting permission for me to "enter through the hatch," He asked, "Major Heaney, this is the top school for a Marine Major. What could you be doing that is more important than attending class with your fellow officers?" I responded, "Conjugal visits to Maryland, Sir!" One of my best military years was at Quantico. I gained tremendous admiration and genuine respect for the Marines, Navy, Air Force and Coast Guard. I thought the demands of a paratrooper were tough, but being a Marine, turning circles in heavy seas waiting for all the landing craft to push away from their Navy ships has to be the toughest. During that year I enjoyed reminding my Marine Corps friends that the Army pulled off the largest beach invasions in history. I enjoyed reminding my Navy friends that the Army transportation corps has more ships than most navies. I also enjoyed sharing with my Air Force friends that the XVIII Airborne Corps had the 6th largest air force in the world.

My cabal from Marine Corps Command and Staff College not withstanding, I worked extremely hard during my military career, consistent with the step necessary to reach my goal. Years later, when I became the G1/AG of the 82nd Airborne Division, I worked hard not so much to attain my goal, but because the commanders and troopers deserved my full dedication. I started the job in May, 1999 after an hour overlap with the outgoing G-1. I didn't take off a day for the entire summer. I was frocked to Lieutenant Colonel by General McNeill, an outstanding paratrooper, in September 1999 with Ted Westhuesing. I asked Ted to share the ceremony with me partly because he was the Division G-3, but mostly because I knew lots of folks would attend to see Ted get frocked. Everybody loved Ted. Ted and I were selected to our respective division staff positions years ahead of our contemporaries. We would get together and commiserate about how difficult our jobs were. Ted was replaced by another incredible leader, Jimmy Huggins, a Major General today. I stuck around in the job for two years. We joked that at least we'd be getting fired from really great jobs.

The wee hours before the ceremony I worked until about 1:00 AM on the Division Unit Status Report (USR). I would have to present the personnel portion of the report to the commanding general earlier the day of our frocking ceremony. I got home too late to pick up my mother at the train station. Thankfully, my wife picked her up, but my absence did not sit well with Mom. She waited up for me and scolded me for missing her train. I scolded her for not helping me with the USR. The next day, just before the ceremony, General McNeill asked one of my mentors to talk to me about "relaxing in the harness a bit" or paratrooper speak for taking some time off. General McNeill knew I'd keep going full steam if I heard that advice from him directly. I followed his advice and took off the Saturday and Sunday after the ceremony. That frocking ceremony on the 82D Airborne Division Headquarters patio stands out of one as my best days in the Army. Today, the memory is bitter sweet because, sadly, Ted died in Iraq. He was a better officer than me.

Ten years later I'm enjoying dinner by the dock at the Wrightsville Yacht Club with the mentor who passed General McNeill's advice to "relax in the harness" Les Bowen. We recalled that day and laughed. Les, a Vietnam War and Gulf War veteran and Purple

Heart recipient said, "Ken you're doing really well now with your investment practice. You've got it made." I responded, "Thanks. It wouldn't be so sweet if it weren't for all those years in the Army. It would be a kind of hollow success." I share these accounts with you because they are indelibly woven into my tapestry of success and will be in yours too. I've benefited from the tremendous opportunity the military afforded me and affords you as well.

The goal I set in 1985 and the professional steps and financial steps to get there helped me to be able to identify challenges and opportunities along the way.

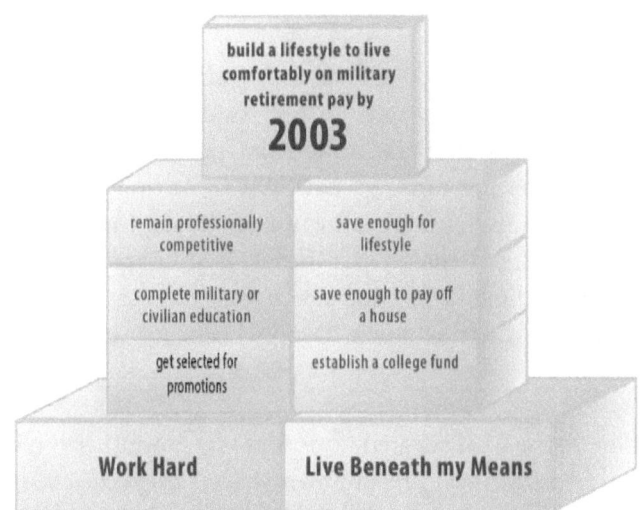

Sit with your family and talk about what long term goals you want to achieve. It may be financial independence during retirement, an Ivy League education for the kids, or anything you want and find important. Then add the steps necessary to make it happen. Without goals, there will be no way to measure success. You can write them in over my goals and steps.

Establish Your Timeline

Next to goal setting, establishing a timeline is critical. It helps to look at life in blocks of time. I was first introduced to the timeline idea by a fellow officer at Fort Bragg. He showed me his professional timeline. It spanned 30 years. He had filled it in with due course promotion dates and military and civilian schooling, and required branch qualifying jobs. Looking at his timeline it became obvious that there was only limited time and space to do career enhancing jobs in order to stay competitive. Thinking about one's military career of 20 years or even beyond, it seems like an eternity to get all the jobs one needs or wants. The reality of it is that the time passes in a blink of an eye. The last five years of my 20 year military career blazed by in a whirl.

The same applies to your financial timeline. It is widely believed that a small investment early in life trumps a larger investment late in life. I hear it all the time from people who wished they had started investing early. So start now by setting your goals and establishing your financial timeline. As you imagine major life events like promotions, retirement, kids in college, military retirement and social security eligibility it becomes clear that life passes too quickly and that there is not as much time to invest for the future as we would like.

With all the sophisticated investment tools out there on various financial websites, including our own, ***mymilitarymillionaire.com*** and ***kennethheaney.com***, I still fall back on a hand drawn timeline when talking about investments, insurance, retirement and taxation with my clients. So let's get started on your own financial timeline. I've started one for you with major life events added:

Life & Financial Events Timeline
(Hypothetical)

"life is like tuition – some pay a little, some pay a lot."
– Ken Heaney

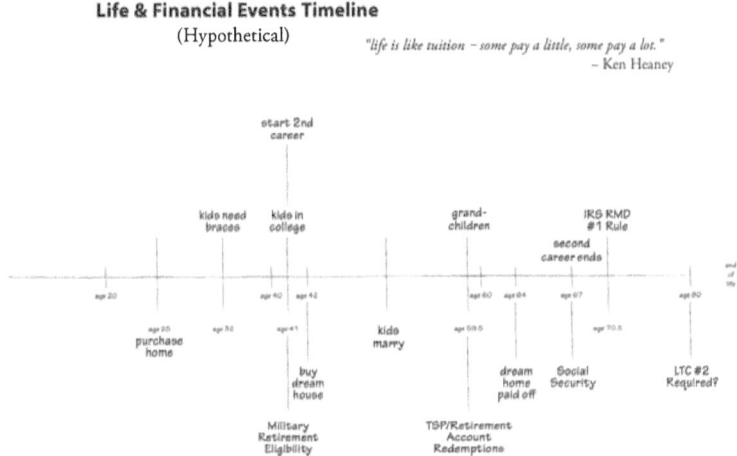

When we look at all the life events that are common to most military families, you can see the time to invest and prepare for the future can be surprisingly short. You may feel that you're already behind in establishing goals and a timeline. Don't be like one of my Army buddies who always said "the sooner I get behind, the more time I have to get caught up!"

Now that you're aware of the building blocks you need to help you think about your financial wellbeing, you're ready to get started. Get your family involved and begin!

Chapter Three

Saving

If you would be wealthy, think of saving as well as getting.
--Benjamin Franklin

It's not what your make, it's what you save. More than 200 years ago, American founding Father Benjamin Franklin said in a sentence what it will take me a chapter to do. Saving is the underpinning of personal wealth. If you're not in the mindset to step up your saving habits, there's no need to read further. If you're not willing to take on board the saving habit, then I can't help you. But, if you want to buy a house someday, you'll need savings to make the down payment. If you want to participate in an investment plan, again you'll need to save first. Want to pursue higher education? Again, you'll need savings to get started. Want a loan? you'll likely need to demonstrate assets in savings. Want to start your own business? You may need to be like me and have saved the venture capital.

Regardless of how much you make, saving is a great habit, not just for yourself, but for your children. I'm about half way through my life time, but I'm pretty sure saving will be a life time habit with me. It's never too early to teach your children the value of putting something aside for the future. When I did the television segment for the Early Show, I was pleased that CBS ended the interview with a shot of our 3 year old putting spare change in his piggy bank. Josh is now a teenager and an avid saver. He's already saved and invested thousands of dollars that can be used toward his college education or later on for purchasing a house or even starting his own business. Josh definitely gets his saving and entrepreneurial spirit from his parents.

Saving is the key to wealth. And living below one's means is the key to saving. When potential clients meet with me for financial strategies, they are often shocked when I tell them they are not living below their means and saving enough. All have great reasons why they spend so much of their income. Many even spend much more than their income. This applies to folks of all income levels. *I've spoken to many affluent looking folks who have less in savings than my teenager son!* Let's be clear: I'm not saying we should live *within* our means. I'm saying we should live well *below* our means. How much below? I believe at least 20 percent below our means. As a culture, Americans are spenders not savers. This is an attribute of our culture that we need to turn around. There is so much pressure on each of us to spend that it's much easier to say than do. I've seen statistics that few Americans even save as little as five percent of their disposable income. That's savings of what remains after the bills are paid. In contrast, I've seen statistics that suggest that the Chinese save as much as 50% of their disposable income. When I think of the future of the world economy, we will likely be yielding to the Chinese as the dominant culture. Most economists agree that the 350 million Americans are saving much less than the 1.3 billion Chinese. There will likely be a day in my life time when the Chinese economy converts from an export economy to a consumer economy, When the Chinese savers become spenders, the U.S. will lose its status as the major world consumers and likely driving up the price of the imported goods that we enjoy so much today. At that time, Americans will likely pay much more for the things we import or simply do with out. If you think our current struggling economy is painful; you'd really hate it when we're no longer the most relevant economy in the world. More than ever, saving will be at a premium.

Learning to save is hard to do with all the pressure on us to buy, buy, and buy. If you don't believe me, just look at the commercials that appear during your favorite television show. You're being encouraged to buy everything from lotions that make you soft to pills that make you hard! And everything is available on easy credit terms. Even President Bush during his firs term urged us to be patriotic and spend more to help pull the country out of recession. It wasn't always this way. If you're like me and enjoy listening to radio shows from the 1940s there was an abundance of commercials asking Americans to actually *save*—including saving money for U.S. war bonds, saving fuel, saving oil and grease for military use and even saving seeds to grow Victory Gardens!

It is true, our parents and grand parents were savers and worked incredibly hard to give us a better life. If you have any doubt about this find someone who is in their 80s and ask them what it was like in the 1920s and 1930s. And we do have better lives but along the way we've learned some very bad habits. The fact is that we're a nation of consumers in a consumer economy. The fuel of the American economy is consumer spending. We as a nation need to turn this around and find a way to fuel the economy without Americans needing to mortgage there future by borrowing and spending instead of saving. Really, learning to save is a matter of getting rid of the bad habit of spending too much. Someone once said, "Bad habits are like a comfortable bed—easy to get into and hard to get out of." But if we can replace the bad habit of spending too much and starting to save then the habit of saving will become our "comfortable bed."

How much should one save? I can't say for you, but for our house hold we try to save 20 percent of our income. *Not disposable income, but total income.* Our savings plan divides our savings into 7 buckets including: a savings account for short term liquidity, Erika's 401(K), my retirement plan, Josh's educational savings plan, investments, life insurance and finally charitable contributions. We have 6 separate savings buckets to contribute to each month *before* we spend what we make. Some months, it's really tough to do, but we always get it done and chose to save before spending. For me, saving has been a life long habit that my parents instilled in me. I've become comfortable with saving and become uncomfortable if I do not save. The feeling of discomfort is a lot like not wearing a seat belt, or wearing an improperly rigged parachute harness. *It just doesn't feel right not to save.* Have you become too comfortable in your spending habits? Are you like the paratrooper who was unwilling to save even 25 dollars a month for a savings bond?

If you're having trouble saving then you're in good and plentiful company. Our government spends far more that it receives in tax revenue. In the Troubled Asset Relief Plan or TARP, the government spent billions of dollars to save General Motors. We spent billions of dollars to save a company whose valuation is reportedly to be $50 million dollars. Government has a twisted way of saving that I find too common in military households. The twisted way of looking as saving is to consider assets not spent as saving. For instance, if government spends $100 million on a program, instead of a projected cost of $200 million, government will report it saved $100 million. Military families too often do the same. We think that spending less for something is the same as saving.

When I worked as an executive officer at the Defense Information Systems Agency, we had an annual budget of about $2 billion dollars. I sat in on many briefings where project officers would report "saving millions of dollars" by spending hundreds of millions of dollars. It used to bother me that we institutionally confused spending a little less with saving. Even today, when I go through a check out line at the grocery store and the cashier tells me "you saved $14.98 by shopping with us," I usually reply something like, "No, I just spent $120." Just because our government and culture is confused by what it means to spend or save, it does not mean we need to fall into this trap, and bad habit.

So if you're not habitually saving from every paycheck then set yourself a goal to do so starting right now! If you're not already saving, start by trying to save just 5percent of your total income. If you make $2000 per month, then try to save $100. It may not seem like much, but saving $100 per month will yield $1200 in savings plus any accrued interest in a year. That's $1200 that you would have not otherwise had.

Are you not sure how to stop spending in order to make saving a habit? Here are some suggestions of how to cut back on your spending and find at least $100 per month:

Put away your savings first, before paying bills. Then establish a budget with what's left over. Saving is contagious. The habit of saving a little will be come easier and easier over time to where you're saving more than you ever thought possible.

Spend less on entertainment. If you go to the movies twice a month, go once and rent a movie and make popcorn at home instead. **You'll save $25 per month.** Go to the library and borrow the movies for free and you'll save even more.

Park the car and walk or peddle. I like to ride my bike the 8 mile round trip to the post office. **By walking or peddling to your errands or work periodically you can easily save $20 per month in gas and you'll probably be healthier for it. My best Army friend, Tommy Seamands, is a general who routinely peddles to the Pentagon for work.**

Prepare meals at home. According to a report by the Bureau of Labor and Statistics the average house hold spends nearly as much on meals prepared away from home as meals prepared at home. Make your own breakfast and lunch. Save dining out for special occasions. **Avoid going out for one breakfast, lunch and dinner a month and save $45.**

Steer clear of the coffee shop. The average coffee shop latte costs about $3.30. It costs about $.20 to brew it yourself. **Skip a trip to the coffee shop per week and save $12.00 per month.** Brew it yourself and save a *latte!*

These are some easy habits most of us can employ to save more than $100 per month.

As an investment professional, I'm always talking with people about their spending and saving habits. I never met a person who could not carve out some savings from his or her financial circumstances. I meet people all the time who are in hock up to their eyeballs and swear they can't save a dime. Here's a story of someone who should of saved but didn't with terrible consequences. I met a lady at Fort Belvoir, Virginia, who did a lot of business providing rental cars to government agencies. She worked for a major car rental agency and made about $75,000 from her job and about $10,000 more from a separate part time job. She was a single parent and owned a modest home in Northern Virginia. She asked me what she could do to better her financial position since she had no savings. After listening to her story, I suggested she stop visiting the coffee shop where she spent more than $100 per month and start an aggressive savings plan as a hedge against the difficult economy. I suggested she return the $1000 HDTV she had just purchased and to save the money instead. I also suggested she sell her car and save the payment, repairs and insurance expense since she was provided a company car. Finally, I suggested she cease dining out until she had built up her savings. I recommended saving $30,000 to $40,000 in case of a down turn in the economy. Unfortunately she did not follow any of my suggestions. Even worse, her position with her employer was eliminated and she lost her job and eventually she lost her home. This is not an uncommon story with record numbers of Americans losing their homes to foreclosure.

The sad thing is the lady who lost her job and home because she felt like she needed the trips to the coffee shop, the HDTV, meals out and the rest. That's a common problem for many Americans who don't know the difference between what they *want* and what they *need*. I learned early in life that obtaining the things I *wanted* were useless unless I had the things I *needed*. Before purchasing anything, and I do mean anything, we should ask ourselves "do I really need this?" I remember reading a story in the news about a young man who fell upon tough financial times because he lost his job. He lost his job because he was routinely late for work. He was late for work because his car was not reliable. He felt the cause of his problems was the car dealer who sold him an unreliable car. The car was a Lamborghini! It was the young man's dream car, but he couldn't afford to maintain it let alone actually drive it. He always *wanted* a Lamborghini, but what he needed was a Honda, or a Toyota, or any reliable economy car. And this jackass really thought his troubles were caused by the car dealer. There was a time that natural selection would have weeded out primates like this, but not today. So know the difference between what you need and what you want. Take care of your needs and you'll find your wants to be less important.

In the military, besides not thinking about the difference between what we need and what we want, we do think of our jobs as being recession proof and that can dampen the urgency and frequency in which we save. But before you get too comfortable with your recession proof career, keep in mind that the military is not immune to downsizing. After the Vietnam War, the military drastically downsized and thousands of service men and women were asked to leave military service. During my own military career, the military downsized significantly in the mid 1990s. The Army whittled down my year group, YG 1983, by 51 percent. Most of my year group was asked to leave during this period. It's unlikely for the near future, but as the Obama administration seeks ways to fund its initiatives and new programs, the military may be asked to downsize again.

How big should your savings account be? It depends on your own financial situation and goals. I'd be happy to discuss this with you personally. You can contact me through our website: www. mymilitarymillionare.com. I can tell you that I don't know anyone who has too much in savings. At any one time, my family keeps $50,000 to $100,000 in savings, *not* counting investments. We have reasons for keeping so much in savings. First I like to keep some cash on the sidelines for buying opportunities in the stock market. More importantly, we make mortgage payments on three separate homes and if anything would happen to me, those payments will continue for many months before my wife would have to start making payments on her own. We use savings to create a buffer in time until my life insurance policies would be paid or until my wife could sell some of the properties. Finally, we keep our savings relatively high to take advantage of buying opportunities with major purchases in cars, appliances and the like. I believe I'm able to work better deals because I could afford to pay cash when a major purchase is necessary. In fact, besides being able to cut an awesome deal on our last new car purchase, the dealer was so anxious to get our cash that he had the car delivered to our house!

After you get the saving habit down to second nature there are some additional steps you can take saving to the next level. I've done all of these since I first joined the Army and continue today. Consider saving a portion of all sources of additional income you receive. For instance, when I was promoted to captain, I continued to maintain a standard of living at the rank of lieutenant. I continued this practice of maintaining a standard of living one rank below my pay grade through my promotion to lieutenant colonel and even later as a GS-14 civil servant. When you get a promotion raise, plan to save half and spend half. When you get a time in grade raise, again, plan on saving half and spending only half. When you get a TDY disbursement, try saving it. When you execute a permanent change of station move, save at least half of your dislocation allowance and travel settlement payment. If you get a tax refund, save at least half. Are you being deployed to an area subject to the combat zone tax exclusion? Save all of the tax exclusion.

A little bit of savings can add up over a lifetime. You can go to our website: www.mymilitarymillionaire.com for free access to the Learning Center where you will find calculators to show you hypothetically how much you can save over time. As a hypothetical, if you save $100 per month in a savings account at a modest 3 percent return, you'll have $32,244 in 20 years (before taxes of course.) That's more than $32,000 you can accrue during the course of a 20 year career. Can you save $200 per month? That will accrue over $64,000 over the course of a 20 year military career. Who can't save $200 per month and who can't use $64,000 at retirement? Saving a little early on and for a long period of time beats trying to save a lot late in life. I have many clients who are retired military and are making six figures in their second career who still wish they had learned the saving habit earlier on in their lives. Some are still finding it very difficult to do so later in life.

So how about getting started with a serious savings program. If you're not saving anything now, try the $100 per month challenge. Take $100 per month from your pay and put it in a Federal Deposit Insurance Corporation (FDIC) insured savings account. Get your children in on the saving habit by asking them to save some of their allowance or earnings. They are never too young to open a joint account with a parent. You can bet that my son had one before he was old enough to go to school! Serving the military and your country already makes you a great example of patriotism to your children. How about instilling a sense of frugality, financial responsibility and financial independence by showing your children that you're a saver and by helping them to become savers too? And if you're already saving at least $100 per month, work toward saving 20 percent of your total income. Benjamin Franklin and 1.3 billion Chinese can't be wrong, can they?

Chapter Four

Bad Debt and Expensive Hobbies

Just because you have it doesn't mean you have to spend it!
Chad Johnson, AKA Ocho Cinco, NFL player

Earning a reported $11 million per year, Chad Johnson is among the highest paid wide receivers in the NFL. Even so, he's stingy with the way he spends his money. On a shopping spree for new earrings, he purchased cubic zirconias rather than real diamonds. When asked why one of the richest players in the game would buy CZs he answered "Just because you have it doesn't mean you have to spend it,"--wise advice! Bad debt is one of the tragedies of our contemporary American and military culture. And it's an age old practice of borrowing and lending. I'm sure the first caveman who invented the wheel, lent it to another caveman at an oppressive interest rate—much like today's credit card companies. Bad debt can turn a family's personal finance into an abyss of hopelessness.

Many Americans and especially service members assume debt too casually. "Spend now and pay later" is a common mantra and inducement. The problem with this rationale is that instead of paying once you could be paying continuously. I'm amazed to see how many of my military friends are shackled to a ball and chain of debt, and bad debt permeates all ranks. I think everyone would benefit from taking a more business-like and skeptical approach before assuming *any* debt, whether it be to buy a car with a personal loan or groceries with a credit card.

I'm not totally against debt. In fact I'm paying on about $1 million in home mortgages. But I did not assume those mortgages lightly or without careful and deliberate forethought. Furthermore, I can underwrite my own debt by substantial investments and life insurance should the unexpected occur. The $1 million in mortgages are backed by a significant personal financial portfolio, half a million dollars in home equity, a significant retirement income, a dual family income, a business ownership, and life insurance. If I were to lose my ability to earn an income, I still have my retirement income. If I lost my life, my insurance would cover the debt. If my wife lost her job, our investments would make up the pay differential. In short, I have loans that I can personally underwrite in one form of another. I can add that my mortgages are the only debt I have with an interest charge. There are no car loans, college loans, credit card debt or any other form of debt that carries an interest charge. Let me repeat this point—aside from my home mortgages, which provide me with a tax break, I carry no debt where there is an interest charge.

The reason home mortgages can be *good debt* is that one can benefit financially from the debt. The principal and interest cost of the mortgages can provide the following tangible benefits:

--A place to live
--Property investment that may appreciate over the long term
--Rental income
--Tax deductions.

Conversely, bad debt, such as credit card debt, is generally not tax deductible and may cost more than the return on investment it may generate. Among my friends is a military family with a six figure income. They've managed to put their three children through college but they don't own their house. They have a significant car loan and credit card debt that takes just about all of their disposable income just to pay the interest charges. Now in their 50s with retirement approaching and very little savings, my friends are facing a financial crisis with significant implications for their emotional well-being. They have almost no nest egg to retire upon, but they do have a Harley Davidson motorcycle. Their plight is way too common and totally unnecessary. This is one of the main reasons I started this book—to help out anyone I can, anyway I can.

You're the Household CFO

Take a business approach when considering taking on debt. In the corporate world, the Chief Financial Officers (CFO) are charged with managing the corporate debt. Corporations assume debt to fund operations and expand productivity. There's a cost analysis and if the cost of the debt is more than the potential gain, the project is normally scrapped. If corporations manage their debt well they flourish. If they don't then they may end up like Enron, AIG, Chrysler or GM. We should all think of ourselves as our household's Chief Financial Officer in this same manner. I've done some cost of debt analysis for some of my friends and it amazes me how one can be presented a model to most efficiently structure debt, yet it may go largely ignored. Here's a hypothetical example of a recommendation to structure debt associated with a school loan:

"Thank you for the opportunity to provide you with some options regarding your student loans. We should have a detailed conversation to discuss the following options that I believe you may want to consider.

Consider obtaining a home equity loan, at a lower interest rate, to pay off the student loans for approximately $98,000. Assuming a fixed interest rate of 7.25%, if you applied the same $1200 per month you are currently applying against the student loan now, you would have 7 fewer payments, and save $8725 in interest over the life of the loan (I provided loan payment calculations to show my math).

Based on your federal income tax rate, there would be an additional benefit of a tax savings associated with the home equity loan interest payment for approximately $2400 the first year with the interest tax deduction declining over the term of the loan based on current tax code."

In this hypothetical, Ben would save approximately 7 fewer loan payments of $1200 for a total of $8,400 and save approximately $2,400 on taxes, with the tax savings decreasing over time. You would think it would be a no-brainer to restructure this debt, but often such suggestions are ignored. (Hypothetical example used for illustration only. Actual results may vary).

Credit Card Debt

Credit card debt is normally debt of the worst kind. To me, there is little financial value in acquiring credit card debt that is not paid off monthly. Credit card legislation may allow issuers to eliminate the grace period before interest accrues. If this occurs with my credit card, I will cut it up and only use cash. Currently, my household puts about $3000 on credit cards each month. But, our cardinal rule is that we pay it off each month in full to avoid a finance charge. I cannot remember the last time I paid a credit card finance charge. It probably last happened to me maybe 25 years ago or maybe longer. Our credit cards have become an asset, because I get immediate purchase power, float time on the monthly charges and rewards from the credit card bank, all for free. Credit card issuers can allow this because they charge merchants a fee for accepting the charge. Even though the credit issuers don't make a cent from me, they make billions from merchants.

Maintaining a balance on your credit card will eventually result in finance charges that more than negate any reward program the card company may offer. *I am not sending you mixed signals.* **My rule is that I never make any charges that I cannot pay off before interest accrues. I pay no credit card interest. I believe in most circumstances, neither should you. Even if your credit**

card offers some reward such as cash back, airline miles or some other incentive.

There's a dark side to those convenient little plastic cards. First, it's the fine print. I've never seen a contract with anything positive for me in fine print. You'll rarely find anything positive for you in fine print. That's why I always, always, read the fine print. Let's look at the fine print associated with one popular credit card.

Did you know that the "no interest cash advance" may come at a cost? Check out the fine print. "Cash advance fee: 3% of the amount of the cash advance, but not less than $5. Late payment fee: $29 if your balance at the time of the late payment is assessed is less than $1000, $35 if your balance at that time is greater than or equal to $1000. Over-the-credit-limit fee: $29." (Source Capital One Small Business Solutions Important Disclosures and Terms of Offer brochure). All I can ask is "Huh?"

One of my clients did an admirable job of climbing out of the credit card debt pit. She had come to me with this question: "Ken, I'd like to retire from teaching in the next five years, but I have credit card debt, a car loan and I've taken several lines of credit on my home loan. I can't make ends meet on my teacher's income now. How can I make it when I'm retired on a reduced retirement income? I have virtually no savings and Social Security won't make up the difference between my current income and my retirement income."

We immediately began a systematic approach to changing her saving and spending habits. My client cut up her credit cards. Cutting up the cards made it difficult to spend frivolously. She paid off the credit cards first since they had the highest interest rate. Then, when she had the cards paid off, she started to save and invest relatively conservatively. Later, she paid off her car and her home. She was able to retire at the time of her choosing and now leads a comfortable life. Why would anyone want to jeopardize their retirement dreams for the sake of short term and often unnecessary purchases? Benjamin

Franklin was prophetic when he said "Beware of little expenses. A small leak will sink a great ship." What are we teaching our children when they see us pull out our credit cards to pay for items we may not be able to afford. Are we teaching them to keep their finances in ship shape? In my own family, my teenage son has had a saving account, a checking account and two mutual funds. He tracks, but does not invest yet in several stocks. He does not have a credit card! He handles many transactions in cash because expenditures seem more real if actual currency is passing from wallet. He's learned from watching his parents. Your children are learning from you. Are they learning the right spending habits?

Believe me, I'm not suggesting that credit cards can't be a useful tool to improve one's quality of life. In the last couple of years, I've received reimbursement for an airline ticket, several free resort stays and hundreds of dollars in cash back from my credit cards. But, I would waive all that if I had to pay a cent in interest. I spend with the cards only what I can afford to pay. None of the rewards are worth paying high credit card interest.

90 Days Same As Cash

I know you've heard of offers such as this. They can be a good deal or a disaster waiting to happen. I'm currently engaged in a "1-year same as cash" purchase from a major building materials supplier. Essentially, I bought $15,000 worth of cabinets and granite counter tops, but the amount will be due in 1-year without interest. But, I generally keep $25,000 sitting in a fund yielding about a 5% income distribution rate. At the end of the year, my $25,000 should grow to an estimated $26,250 and from that I will pay off my cabinet bill.

However, if for some reason I could not pay off the entire $15,000 I'd be liable for 12% interest for the whole year! My $15,000 cabinets and granite counter tops would cost me $16,800. That would blow. So beware of "same as cash deals." If you don't have the cash put away somewhere relatively easily accessible, such as a bank certificate of deposit-- you may be setting yourself up for a serious interest smack-down.

Make your hobbies pay their own way.

Sometimes, perhaps too often, I see folks around me with expensive hobbies that keep them from achieving financial freedom or at least financial peace of mind. It doesn't matter what your hobby is. Whether it's collecting stamps or the latest electronic gadgetry, horseback riding or lawn tractor racing, collecting wine or drinking beer, it can be very detrimental to your financial future. Your hobby's cost can keep you from reaching a more secure place.

Horse Sense

I know folks who are into horses. All things equestrian are their passion and hobby. Some even call their hobby a business. But in my mind, it's a hobby, not a business. Why not a business? It's because many of those have never shown a profit from their "horse business." They aren't trying to run some sort of exotic tax shelter. They really lose a lot of money from their horse hobby. How much money? Lots of money, easily tens of thousands of dollars a year are lost. Now that's an expensive hobby.

Some of these "horse people" have shared their financial status with me and it's often not impressive. It's scary. You see, too many are in hock up to their eyeballs, due mostly because of his hobby. Typically, the house and farm are mortgaged close to or even beyond their market value with virtually no equity. Most of the horse stock has little or no marketable value. They don't own their cars or farm machinery and their credit cards are overloaded. And even though some do not have children, given their current investment picture, they will likely never be able to retire from their full time jobs without taking up second jobs or severely reducing their current lifestyle.

I have owned many horses and understand that horses can be part of the family. Horse people love their horses. However, horses can be a drag on a household's finances like no other hobby. With what other hobby can you buy a $750,000 farm, $40,000 in horse fencing, a $40,000 truck, a $10,000 horse trailer to transport a $700 nag to a horse show to win a 75 cent fourth place ribbon at a B rated horse show? Wouldn't it be more cost effective to just buy a blue first place ribbon for a dollar or so and pretend it was won at a horse show? Wouldn't it be easier just to burn the money and save the trouble of cleaning up the horse poop in the field? I've got to admit that my wife is an accomplished equestrian and we've owned horses over the years. There are four horses on my farm in North Carolina. But she's managed to enjoy her hobby fairly inexpensively by buying used tack, buying less expensive horses and doing a lot of her own horse chores. Unfortunately, many horse people are deeply in debt because their hobby is so expensive.

I've seen similar circumstances with boat owners. They say the two happiest days for the boat owner are the day he buys the boat and the day he sells it! My own brother is a boater. He often jokes about how much his boat costs, even when it's not in the water. Instead of buying a boat, consider renting or chartering a boat. For one of my boat owning clients, I calculated he could charter a boat for the 5 or so times he goes out on the water and save thousands of dollars a year. Not even counting the cost of the boat, insurance, fuel, taxes, maintenance, registration, docking and storage were costing a small fortune.

There's nothing wrong with an expensive hobby if that's your idea of the pursuit of happiness, but why mortgage your future, with all the angst and anxiety that goes with it? Because at the end of the game, the end of life all we have are two things: dignity and choices. If you're not financially fit, your choices will be few and your dignity will be compromised. You don't believe me? Who has more choices and dignity in life, Hugh Hefner or a guy in line at your local mission? Of course it's Hugh Hefner, surrounded by a beautiful home, beautiful people and lots of help. You may not agree with his moral compass but the dignity and choices available to him are undeniable. Horror novel author and icon Stephen King wrote "it's a bitch the last years of your life are spent getting old." Rather than being a "bitch," old age can be a blessing and the golden times of one's life, but only with dignity and choices that come with a golden rocking chair. So why would one jeopardize the last years of their life by pursuing a hobby that diminishes their financial fitness is a wonder to me. But people do it all the time. And too often the satisfaction they receive from their hobby is hollow. A hobby that robs one of their financial security and ultimately one's dignity and choices in the final years of life is a horror story in my book and totally avoidable. And if you're in danger of this, I'll tell you how not to end up a victim in this horror story. How about making your hobby pay for its self? I have one hobby I do for the simple joy and enjoyment of the hobby—old cars. I can't say just collecting old cars because my hobby is bigger than that. I love all kinds of old cars and have found many, many, many ways to enjoy my hobby without spending a bundle of money and if I did a thorough accounting, and my hobby probably not only pays for itself, but probably makes a little money. I'm always looking for old car bargains and enjoy shopping for new acquisitions to my garage as I do driving my old cars. My current old car project is a 1963 International Scout 80. If you're not familiar with the car it's one of the nation's first true all wheel drive cars. It looks sort of like an old Bronco and is a kick to drive, especially with the top off.

It runs better than it looks!

I bought it for about $2500 and do as much as the maintenance that it requires that I can myself. I bought the Scout with the proceeds from the 1967 Cadillac Deville convertible I sold. I bought the Cadillac with the proceeds from the 1963 Ford Falcon I sold. I bought the Falcon with the proceeds from the first 1967 Cadillac Deville Convertible I sold. You get the point. I especially enjoy the Scout because it was inexpensive to acquire and it's four cylinder engine is relatively fuel efficient for a car of it's age. And keep in mind there wasn't much incentive for cars to be fuel efficient back in 1963 when my Scout was build because a gallon of leaded regular was about 20 cents. I have a special decoration I like to put on the front grill and bumper during December and January. It's a tire sized wreath with a small deer stuffed animal perched sitting up in the wreath. It definitely turns heads and I enjoy talking to people who inevitably ask me about the car. When I pass by kids always give me the thumbs up sign which is a lot better than the other hand signal people flash when they have road rage. I think what's most enjoyable about my hobby is that it that it's very inexpensive and puts no financial pressure on my household budget. But besides enjoying driving and maintaining the Scout, I pursue my hobby in other inexpensive ways. I go to several car shows during the year, some of which are free and the expensive ones cost about the same as a couple of games of bowling. At the annual Carlisle, Pennsylvania fall car show, for about $30 I can pay for my admittance, lunch and gas to and from the event and keep me occupied all day. Thirty dollars for a days worth of entertainment is what I call a cheap hobby. Besides car shows, I indulge myself with car magazines. I love reading all sorts of car magazines (in addition to the nine investment journals I read monthly). Most of the local grocery stores carry free car advertisement magazines at the entrance of the store. I always pick up a copy. I also enjoy reading Car and Driver, Motor Trend and Road and Track, free of charge, at my local barbershop. Also, my brother-in-law supplies me with free vintage car magazines that he gets from his brother. No, I'm not cheap. I just like to keep my hobby as inexpensive as possible.

Another example of a cheap hobby of mine is coaching high school football. It's hugely rewarding to see the players learn the game, mature and play as a team. The kids learn life lessons in the game. The season lasts about 20 weeks, about 15 hours per week. I put about $300 of my own money into the sport during the season. So I get 300 hours of entertainment for about a dollar per hour. I don't coach football because it's an inexpensive hobby, but I'm not a professional coach, so I try the keep the hobby inexpensive. And like I mentioned earlier, it's hugely rewarding.

Here's some real-life examples that people have shared that suggest their hobbies are too expensive:

1--A guy spends $400 on skis, boots and poles to save the $25.00 rental fee. The problem is he skis twice a year. It will take 16 years to break even on that acquisition. Stick to renting.

2—A guy buys a $500 kayak. He belongs to a club at a lake with free boats available, but he buys a kayak anyway to "stay fit." The kayak has yet to be in the water. Save the $500 until you're serious about kayaking.

3—A guy buys a $25,000 farm tractor to replace his used tractor because maintenance was costing him too much—about $500 per year. He'll break even in 50 years, not counting the interest on the loan for the tractor.

4—A guy buys a trailer, a log splitter and chain saw at $6,000 to cut his own wood to heat his home. At $75 a cord, and assuming his time is worth $20.00/hour I'm pretty sure his back will give out before he comes close to breaking even.

5—A lady's hobby is shopping, and she manages to spend all the expendible income plus a little bit more each month from her husband's $10,000 monthly income. No kidding. This lady definitely needs a new hobby. They don't own their house, their cars or have any significant liquid assets. They would be better off if she volunteered her time to a worthy cause to cut into her mall time. It would probably provide more personal satisfaction than bargain hunting anyway.

6—A guy buys a $30,000 travel trailer to save $2000 per year on vacation hotel expenses. The math never adds up on this one. If you like to camp, then camp. But try to find a way to keep it cheap. My family camps on average of three times a year. It's lots of fun, even when the weather doesn't cooperate. But to keep it cheap, we rent the camper for about $400 total for all three camping trips. Plus, there's virtually no maintenance, extra insurance or storage costs when we rent. Which is more efficient, $30,000 to buy, or $400 to rent? You decide.

7—A lady buys a $6000 lawn tractor (a really nice one) to cut her 1 acre yard. Of course, the lawn guy will do it for $50.00 a cutting. If she cuts the grass 10 times a season, it will take at least 12 years to break even, discounting her time, the cost of gas and repairs.

One of my favorite expensive hobby stories became apparent while I was vacationing at Wrightsville Beach, North Carolina. Wrightsville is one of the more exclusive beaches in North Carolina. We vacation there every year not so much for the exclusivity, but because my rewards credit card buys me free stays at a resort there. Also, I enjoy running at the beach and especially around the Wrightsville Park. We also dine at the Blue Water Restaurant. Dining there is an incredible experience. It's relaxed, located on a marina where many yachts are moored, with friendly service and exquisite food. While waiting for my dinner to be served, I enjoy walking around the docks and seeing and admiring the large fishing and pleasure yachts. Now boating can be an expensive hobby. I'm always amused when I see a million dollar fishing yacht pull in, that burned about $300 in fuel for the day so the owner can catch about $25 in sea bass. I can begin to calculate how much that sea bass cost per pound. Unless one is fabulously wealthy, chartering a boat would be much less expensive. Heck, going to fish market and just buying the sea bass would be more cost effective. Like I mentioned earlier, I truly admire the yachts. My brother is a boat owner and he frequently tells me it would be easier to just burn the money it takes to keep the boat in the water.

Now hear is some examples of people who keep their hobbies cheap, and smart:

1 — A guy needs a new convertible top for his project car. He gets an estimate of $2500 for a shop to remove the old top, fabricate and install a new top. Instead, he buys a new top from a catalog for $125. He borrows a free video on how to

remove a convertible top and removes it himself at no cost. He hires a worker from the shop who provided the estimate to do the job for $25 per hour on the side and the guy helps out. It took him 5 hours at $25 per hour for a cost of $125. The $2500 top cost 250 and eight hours of his own time. Now that's being thrifty and smart!

2 — A guy needs a new rear end for his 1963 Scout after busting his axle (any idea who this is?) He finds a rebuilt axle across the country for $800, plus shipping, plus installation. Instead, he buys a 1963 Scout parts car for $400, doesn't pay shipping, finds a mechanic who has a soft spot in his heart for old Scouts and get the job done for another $400 and still has the parts car for other parts.

3 — A young lady who is college bound takes Advanced Placement English, Math, Biology and Spanish and obtains 12 college credits for about $200 saving her family about $6000 in college tuition for those same credits. Now that's smart!

4 — A guy who needs to have his home heating system replaced at a cost of $6000 makes an agreement to have the work done for only $4000 and he assists the HVAC installer saving $2000 and getting a working knowledge of the system.

5 — A Certified Public Accountant agrees to barter her tax preparation experience for free horse board.

6 — A lady who likes to garden, rather than pay a service $3,000 to install an irrigation system, hires a golf course greens keeper to do it as a side job for less than $1000.

7 — This is one of my favorites. A wealthy retired lady who loves touring homes obtains her realtor's license and becomes a successful realtor in her spare time. This lady was quite wealthy before becoming a realtor but was smart enough to

find a way to finance her hobby. Now her hobby generates income and legitimate tax write offs.   And by the way, this lady did not become wealthy from inheritance, or a one in a million investment scheme, or a fabulous income over a long period of time. She and her husband did it by making careful, thoughtful and sound financial decisions over a lifetime!

I love to talk to people about their hobbies and I'm always surprised to hear how expensive they can be. If you have a hobby and want some suggestions on how to make it more affordable, send me an email note at Kenneth.heaney@natplan.com and I'd be happy to share my thoughts with you.

You can take Chad Johnson's advice that "just because you have it doesn't mean you have to spend it," or simply take my advice and do the math an find out how much that loan is really costing you and what it could cost you if you don't meet the terms. Whatever works for you! If Chad Johnson, who will likely make move than $100 million during his NFL career can temper his spending and borrowing habits, you can too.

Chapter Five

Keep the Cash and the Clunker

"Sometimes your best investments are the one's you don't make."
Donald Trump

As much as I enjoy automobiles, they can be a real drag on your financial future if not carefully purchased and maintained. I know too many folks who have never owned their car title. It's been owned by the bank. However, they do own the car loan. In many cases, it is better to own your vehicle than make payments on an auto loan. Car payments are number two on my list of bad debt, right behind credit card debt. An average of 17 percent of the house hold budget goes to automobile related expenses. (Source: Autoweek) Wouldn't it be great to be able to keep some of that 17 percent for yourself? right behind credit card debt. Why would anyone think it's a good idea to buy a new car which will depreciate three or four thousand dollars in value as soon as the buyer drives it off the lot? I'll give you some tangible ways to avoid the new car and auto loan traps.

Yugo My Way

When I was a lieutenant, my peers jeered because I drove a 1987 Yugo. At the time I reminded my friends that the new car they were riding in was a European sports coupe. Unfortunately, no one believed that my Yugo was any kind of sports coupe. Even worse, none of my friends had the geographical knowledge to actually identify Yugosalvia (the Yugo's namesake) as a European country. Note that neither Yugoslavia nor the Yugo survive today. My friends used to make fun of me for driving a Yugo when they were all driving BMWs, Mercedes, and the like. I was embarrassed to park it at the officers club. My troops used to lift up the car and hide it in the woods near my office for good spirited fun. Nevertheless, it was a very savvy purchase. Why? It's simple. When I bought the Yugo, I set aside my *desires* in favor of and bought using my *needs,* thus taking the long view.

The Yugo was cheap--$5000 or so new with air conditioning. It got terrific gas mileage, 45 MPG highway, and came with a 3 year warranty. Although my strategy was to sell it as soon as the warranty ran out, I ended up keeping it nearly 5 years because it was so reliable and cheap to keep. My wife asked me to sell it because we were reassigned to Washington, DC and she did not want me jousting with 18 wheelers on the Capital Beltway. Besides the routine maintenance of new tires and brakes, the only extra expensees were a new battery that cost about $35.00 and a $75 muffler repair that was required when I went off road in my Yugo. I nearly beat the $35.00 battery replacement by push starting the car for a year. That's right! I push started the car for a year to save buying a $35.00 battery. Finally, my wife insisted on the new battery after she borrowed my car, didn't park on a down grade as I suggested and found she couldn't push the Yugo briskly enough in high heels to kick start it.

I reluctantly sold the Yugo for $1000 after driving the car for nearly 5 years and 60,000 miles. No trade-in this time. I sold the Yugo at the Fort Bragg Lemon Lot. In fact, I sold it within about an hour of placing it For Sale By Owner. The Yugo cost me about $1000 a year to operate, not counting gas. That's about $3.00 a day! Now that's cheap and finance friendly. Today, you'll have an easier time making a wise car purchase than when I purchased the Yugo because there are so many great and efficient models along with sellers desperate to make deals.

I bought the Yugo new in 1988 for reliable, inexpensive and warranted transportation. I traded my GT Mustang and ego along with it. Because I was not saddled with an expensive car loan like many of my peers who were driving Mercedes and BMWs, I could purchase a house and start investing. Today, I'm still friends with some of my peers from my lieutenant days, but they are not joking anymore. They are asking me for financial advice and are still trying to pay off their cars. The steps for getting a great car deal are simple:

1. Consider what you *need* before what you *want.*
2. Consider the *retail, private sale,* and *trade-in* values.
3. Consider *used* before *new.*
4. Consider a *private* sale before a *dealer* lot.
5. Consider *paying cash* and *avoiding credit.*
6. *Never* buy a car unseen or without a test drive.
7 *Always* sleep on the deal before committing.

Follow these suggestions before committing to a car purchase and you will exponentially increase the odds that you will get a better deal.

The Car Deal of the Century Comes Once a Week

Too many go about their car purchase backwards. They visit car lots looking for a make, model and color that catch their attention. Car dealers descend upon and pressure them to make a purchase. They often try to engage you in a conversation about what car payments you can afford rather than the total cost of the car. My best advice is to reverse the process; and here's how.

First, **know what you're looking for** before you step on a lot or talk to a private seller. Think about how you plan to use the vehicle for 90 percent of the time. Then think of how you can accommodate the other 10 percent of the time. For example, 90 percent of my travel is business related and alone. I travel about 35,000 miles per year by myself in all weather conditions including snow and ice. I often travel in the city. Occasionally, though, my family of 3 travels in my car on vacation. So what I *need* is a car that has front or four wheel drive, gets good gas mileage, is easy to maneuver and park in the city, but can accommodate 3 adults and their baggage for a week long vacation.

Taking my own rules of car buying into account, I purchased a new 2005 Hyundai Tucson. I bought it new from a dealer because few were available for sale by private owners at the time. It gets 21 city MPG and 27 highway MPG on regular unleaded gas. It's small enough to easily maneuver in the city or parking garages. It's large enough to carry my family with most of our luggage. For less than $100 I purchased a roof carrier to handle baggage overflow. It came with a 3-year 50,000 mile bumper-to-bumper warranty and a 5-year 100,000 drive train warranty. I sold my 2003 Suburban privately for $21,000 and bought the Tucson for $21,000. Only taxes and registration fees were due out of pocket. The main reason I traded down from the Suburban to the Tucson was for the improved gas mileage and the warranty. In trading down, I have saved approximately 1400 gallons of gas or $4200. What have I done with the $4200 difference? Invest it of course!

A Volvo and a Pop Tart

Although I'm satisfied with the deal I got on the Tucson, I believe there are even better deals in the used private sale market. Another wise car purchase was my 1991 Volvo GL Sedan with 90,000 miles, which I purchased in 1999 for about $4000 from a used car dealer. The paint was badly spotted with pine tar, the interior fabric was dull, and the automatic transmission wouldn't shift into overdrive, making a 3 speed out of a 4 speed. The dealer wouldn't budge on the price, because the price represented the trade-in expense the dealership had in the car, but its $4000 price tag was well below the book value, even without overdrive. Always check the book value for the car you're planning to buy or sell. You can easily do this by answering a few questions about the car and your location at www.kbb.com.

I took the Volvo to a foreign car specialist where the mechanics wear white lab coats, The "service technician" said the car needed a new transmission, but I could continue to drive it as is until the transmission totally quit and have it repaired later. Unfortunately, the repair would cost nearly as much as I paid for the car. And when it finally broke down, it probably would happen at some remote place where there are no motels. I didn't doubt the foreign car specialist's diagnosis; he did have a white lab coat after all. However, on a whim I got a second opinion from an independent neighborhood garage. The place looked more like a junk yard than the gleaming foreign car specialist's shop. But the sign in front of the shop declaring "Garage" was a little more inspiring. The owner, John, asked me to leave the car with him for a few days and he would give me his opinion.

When I returned to claim the Volvo the bill came to about $100.00 to clean the engine and flush and refill the transmission fluid and clean the transmission screen. This did the trick and the Volvo was back in business with overdrive operating properly. So much for needing a new transmission! I said, "John, thank you very, very much for restoring my overdrive and saving me about $4000. I understand now that flushing the transmission fluid could clean the sensor that tells the transmission to shift into overdrive, but I got to ask what cleaning the engine had to do with fixing the transmission?" "Absolutely nothing," John said. "I just like working on a clean engine."

I repaid John's expertise with a bit of my own. John is a Vietnam War veteran. He told me that he was struggling with some service connected medical issues, but the Veteran's Administration (VA) would not treat him because his military medical record had been lost nearly 25 years earlier. Fortunately, I had worked on a task force to digitize military medical records, to put them on a data base that is visible by all the VA regional offices, as well as streamline Army and VA procedures when processing retiree medical records. I believe the VA is still using the system we developed. After contacting the right office in the VA, we found John's medical record from

Vietnam. When I handed over the record to him, he wept with joy. What a wonderful experience for both of us.

I detailed the interior and exterior of the car. After a day laboring on the Volvo, the interior looked almost like new and the exterior gleamed a blinding deep black. Now my friends joked that I looked like the ambassador of Sweden in the shiny black Volvo. When they found out the Volvo only cost me four bills, the jokes quickly ceased. Friends were asking me to find them a similar deal. Soon after I bought the Volvo, I drove it to a cocktail party. There I engaged in small talk with a man who said he was an IBM executive in charge of notebook computer sales in Europe. He saw me pull up in the Volvo and wanted to tell me he had recently sold a Volvo much like mine. He had sold it because it looked dingy and pockmarked with dozens of pine tar spots blemishing the exterior. Also, he said the transmission did not shift properly. He could hardly believe that my new Volvo was his old Volvo. Small world.

Four years and 80,000 miles later I sadly sold the Volvo at the Fort Bragg Lemon Lot for $4000. I happened to have a life-sized cut out of so called "Pop Tart" Brittney Spears looking hot and sexy with a can of soda in her hand. My nephew had given it to me so I put in my garage where she stayed for years greeting me each time I drove the Volvo into the garage. With some urging from my wife, I agreed to get rid of Brittney. Brittney gave me a great idea to capitalize on her popularity and use her for some shameless marketing. When I took the Volvo to the Fort Bragg Lemon Lot, I put Brittney sitting up in the back seat. The sign read, "FOR SALE, BRITTNEY SPEARS--ONLY $4000 (and I'll throw in the Volvo)."

I got several calls, but two were noteworthy. In the first call, a prospect left a message on my voice mail that he'd give me $2000 cash for the Volvo if he could have it that day. I called him back and said, "Hey, I'll take the $2000 for the Volvo, but you can't have it for a week." The guy asked, "A week? Why can't I have it today?"

"Because it will take me a week to remove the engine," I said. "Surely you don't expect the whole car for $2000."

The next one was even better. I met the prospective buyer at the Lemon Lot. He was middle aged, clean cut and seemed like a decent guy, so I really hoped he'd buy the car since I knew it had a lot of trouble free miles left in it and I wanted it in good hands. And don't forget it came with Brittney Spears! He had traveled from Florida for a short tour of duty at Fort Bragg and he thought the Volvo would be perfect for his college-bound daughter. He agreed to buy it and asked me to remove Brittney and take her with me. I said, "Are you kidding me? You'd make quite an impression on your friends back in Florida when you come home in your new used Volvo with Brittney Spears in the back seat." Again, he asked me to take Brittney with me. Again I asked "Are you serious?" Finally he said, "Look, I'm an ordained minister and my daughter would really like the car, but my congregation would not like to see me driving with Brittney in the back seat." I took Brittney off his hands. So this was a Win-Win-Win situation. I got my $4000, the minister got his Volvo, and K-Fed ended up with Brittney, at least for a while. Again, I drove for four years for nearly free. Now that's a good deal if you can get it. And you can too!

The Art of the Deal

If it's time for you to buy a new or used car, keep in mind there are many great car buys out there for you. And the best part is that the deal of the century comes about once a week in the automobile industry. *You* are buying. *You* have the power. Most likely you can get along without immediately buying a car, but the dealer cannot stay in business long without your cash. The dealer needs you a lot more than you need the dealer.

When it comes to new car shopping, be smart. Be powerful. The first question you should ask yourself is "Do I really need a *new* car rather than a *newer* car?" A 1-year old car will likely have low mileage, a warranty, look and drive like new for thousands less. A great example is the 2000 Ford F-150 I purchased after selling the Volvo. We needed a truck for pulling a horse trailer, camper and hauling hay. Rather than buying new we bought a year old truck. The original sticker price was more than $29,000. I picked it up with 12,000 miles for just $18,500. There's even more to the savings than the obvious $10,500 off the sticker price. Well invested, the $10,500 I saved in 2001 has grown substantially in value in a mutual fund *. So that's why it's worth asking yourself, "Do I really need a new car?" If the answer is "yes" consider what you *need* in that new car, rather than what you *want*.

*Note: No strategy or product can guarantee a profit. Investments will fluctuate with changes in market conditions.

It's simple, yet crucial, to consider your needs versus your wants. If you get what you want, without getting what you need, you'll definitely be having some problems. You'll still have the needs that must be satisfied. However, neglecting your wants in a new car purchase is usually not a long term problem since most folks' wants change over time. A new Mercedes is heaven, better than sex, tremendous—for the first month. It's pretty cool for the first 6-months. But within a year it won't be a big deal. By then you'll probably have discovered a completely different car you'll want instead.

If you need to buy a car I urge you to consider something that has been gently used over new, and preferably from a private seller rather than a dealer because the private seller can normally sell the vehicle for less. If you're determined to buy a new car here are some points to improve your negotiating position. They come from a friend who sells cars at one of the largest automobile dealerships in America:

When you first start to discuss price with the dealer start out by saying "This is not my dream car."

Don't let the dealer get you to negotiate payment. You're more interested in the final price. And if you don't pay cash, the real final price is the car, plus taxes, registration and interest over the life of the loan.

Be prepared to walk away. You have the money and the power. The dealer needs your cash to stay in business, but you don't need the dealer's car to stay in business.

Look for a left over model. You'll get most of the benefits of a new car at thousands less.

Don't get suckered into a bunch of options you don't really need or even want because the dealer happens to have a model on the floor with those options.

Don't be shy about asking for a lower price. What's a good price? I always shoot for paying what the dealer paid minus any incentives. The dealer hold back is sufficient profit in my book. Many dealers will show you their invoice upon request.

Don't allow yourself to be pressured. If you feel any pressure, tell the sales person you'll have to leave.

I'm not suggesting that dealers are not honest or helpful. I've had some very positive experiences with dealers. One of my friends is a car salesman and he's a stand up guy. I am suggesting that you need to be in control and look out for your own interest.

A Saab Story

Here's a sob story, or maybe I should say a SAAB story: Back in 1988 my wife desperately wanted a Saab 900S in Rose Quartz paint with an automatic transmission. When I say desperate, I mean desperate. Like the "Desperate Housewives," but on Red Bull and expresso. I could not talk her into something a little more conventional like a Ford Taurus. Even though the Saab 900S looked like an overgrown cockroach on wheels, nothing else would satisfy her. So I went to the Saab dealer and got within $500 of my maximum price I was willing to pay for a 1988 Saab 900S in Rose Quartz with an automatic transmission. I talked the dealer down to about $21,000, which to me was a lot of money back in 1988, but I didn't really want to pay more than $20,500. At the end of the bargaining to $21,000 I told the salesman, "I'd like to go home and sleep on it and make a decision in the morning." The salesman responded, "Sorry, but this price is only good for today." I returned his calling card and said, "Too bad. I guess I won't be needing your business card." I got up and just walked away. The next week I saw a similar, but used, 1987 Saab 900S in Rose Quartz and with automatic transmission and only

10,000 miles at a used car dealer. I bought that car for $10,500, about half the price of the new one. Today, the $10,500 I saved by buying used is worth almost $43,000 assuming a 7% annual growth.*
* Note: The rate used is for hypothetical illustration only and may not be used to predict investor results.

So walking away can be a smart strategy. There's power in being savvy with your car purchases. The $43,000 I've saved over time by buying the used Saab would be enough for a lot of things in life that are probably more important. For instance, $43,000 would be an ample down payment on a $200,000 house. Or $43,000 would be a tidy sum to fund an individual retirement account. The $43,000 would pay for a state college education in many states or be a nice down payment on a private institution. The point is that a disciplined approach to car buying can save you thousands of dollars and possibly more than a hundred thousand dollars over a lifetime and improving your financial position immensely. Too many car buyers never give this a serious thought.

So you're still not convinced you want to go used for your next car purchase and are desperately craving that new car smell? There's still action you can take to make sure you don't mortgage your financial future to purchase a new car. When shopping for a new car, go into the show room knowing the difference between your *wants* and your *needs*. If you don't satisfy your *wants*, that's ok. They will probably change over time anyway and never be totally satisfied. However, if you don't satisfy your *needs*, you will be troubled, and possibly forced into making another car purchase prematurely. Especially when car manufacturers come out with the next "best thing" every couple of months. You'll have to take my word for this, but "best does not exist." There's just no such thing as best. There's OK, good enough, pretty good and excellent, I'm here to tell you that best just does not exist in the car world. A foolish car purchase can mean disaster for your personal finance.

When considering your next car purchase here's a list of some items you may *want*:

--A prestigious model
--Leather seating
--Quick acceleration
--Spirited handling
--Metalic blue paint

However, here's a list of the items you may *need*:

--Seating for four
--Safety
--Fuel economy
--Reliability
--Long warranty

Now let's see how knowing the difference between your *wants* and your *needs* can make a huge difference in a smart car purchase and your financial future. Here's how two similar cars compare:

	Lexus RX3	Hyundai Tucson
Prestige	Yes	No
Leather	Yes	Yes
Quick Accel	Yes	Yes
Handling	Yes	Yes
Seating	5	5
Mileage	18 MPG	22 MPG
Reliability	Yes	Yes
Warranty	3 Yrs/36K miles	5 Yrs/100K miles
Price	About $46K	About $23K
Smart?	You decide.	

By the way, let's assume you plan to keep either car for four years and your have $23,000 in cash and trade-in. To finance the additional $23,000 at 4% interest for the Lexus over four years would cost your nearly $2000 more in interest, not including a higher sales tax and registration that may be associated with the higher vehicle purchase price.

Check the website, www.mymilitarymillionaire.com, for free help when evaluating the real cost of your next automobile purchase. Click the "Learning Center" tab for auto loan affordability and loan payment calculators that are available to you free of charge.

Coincidentally, often there is a metallic blue Lexus RX parked next to my silver Hyundai at my office. They look so much alike it's surprising, so I smile every time I get behind the wheel of my Hyundai. I've got nothing against the Lexus which is a finely engineed car I'd like to own. I just don't need one, and I suspect that thousands of Lexus owners don't really need theirs either. As a final point, I had stopped for gas on my way back from a business trip. I pulled into a gas station and was parked at the pump next to the driver of a Lexus RX. I remarked to the driver "What a great car. How do you like it?" He replied "Yeah, it's a nice ride, but the 16 miles per gallon I'm getting is killing me. How is your car on gas?" I'm getting about 27 miles per gallon on this trip." "Great! Just great!" he replied. Sure I felt a little smug, but sometimes smug feels a lot better than prestigious.

Trade-in Zen

Before I wrap up my thoughts on cars and your personal finance, I need to say a few words about trading in your old car. According to a friend of mine who works at one of the largest car dealerships in the country, about 90% of new car purchasers trade in their old car. Trading in your old car may be wise or unwise, depending on the situation. Over the years I've owned 20 cars of all kinds, from the economical 1987 Yugo GL to a pair of big 1967 Cadillac Deville Convertibles. However, during that time, I've traded-in only two cars. All the others I sold privately with relative ease. The oldest car I sold was a 1963 Ford Falcon that sold in 1998 and the newest was a1995 Isuzu Rodeo sold in 1997. In each case I sold the cars for considerably more than I would have received from a dealer trade-in. In some cases I sold the cars for even more than my purchase price. The Falcon I sold for twice my purchase price after driving it for several years. One of the Cadillacs I sold for two and a half times the purchase price after driving it four years. I already told you about the Volvo I sold for nearly what I bought it for after driving 70,000 miles.

In the summer of 2003 my wife decided she wanted to trade-in her 1997 Suburban with more than 90,000 miles for a leftover 2003 Suburban. I knew the owner of the GM dealership, whose son went to school with mine. I trusted him and felt like we worked a pretty good price on the 2005 Suburban. In negotiating the price I started out by telling the dealer, "This is not my dream car," just like I advise you to do. The only problem was that the dealer could offer me only $7500 as a trade-in for my old Suburban.

After careful consideration I decided to pay cash for the new Suburban and sell the old Suburban myself. What I had in my favor is that the 1997 Suburban was mechanically sound and in nearly immaculate condition. I even kept the engine compartment detailed. After advertising the car in the local newspaper for just a few days I had my first prospective buyer come to see it. When he and his wife and children returned from a short test drive his wife was absolutely beaming. It was obvious she wanted my car when she told him in from of me, "I want this car. Give him what he wants for it." I looked at the guy and said, "I guess you just lost your bargaining power." He agreed to give me the $12,000 I was asking for the car. End of deal with me up $4500 over what the dealer offered, right? Not exactly. After the buyer agreed to pay the $12,000 I sweetened the deal for him. I reduced the price by $500 saying, "Make your check out for $11,500. The $500 difference is to pay for your first repair. I can't say what that repair will be, but it will come someday and it's important to me for you to feel like you're getting a fair deal. So I'm paying for your first repair up front." The buyer looked amazed, but was very appreciative. I do this with most of the cars I sell myself, especially if I'm asking more than a few thousand dollars for the car. Also, when I'm selling a car myself I always disclose its defects. I believe it's always better to disclose the car's defects rather than have the prospective buyer find out themselves and lose confidence in my honesty and walk away from the sale. If you believe in Karma as I do, then there's no reason to get on the wrong side of it by not disclosing the car's shortcomings. The $4000 I saved by selling my car myself rather than trading it in has grown significantly. Imagine the power of having an additional few thousand dollars more in the bank today by selling your car yourself just a few years earlier. That's a little Zen with which we can all live.

Of the two cars I've traded-in, both cases I lost confidence in the cars mechanically and was not comfortable selling in a private sale. I traded them in and disclosed to the dealers the trouble I was having with them at the time. In one case the car's transmission was slipping requiring an expensive rebuild or even more expensive new transmission. In the other case the car's engine would spontaneously overheat seemingly for no reason at all. With both cars I did not want to saddle a private buyer with these problems and get on the wrong side of Karma.

Zero Financing or Cash Back

Most of us need a reliable car to get to work and there comes a time when we lose trust and confidence in the reliability of our ride so we shop for a new car. I do realize that most folks can't afford to pay cash for their new car but consider the real cost of a loan.

Many auto makers will give you a choice of a factory rebate or zero percent interest on a loan. When shopping for a Suburban we had the choice of a $3000 factory rebate **or** zero percent financing for 36 months, on a $33,000 loan but not both. Which would you take, the rebate or the financing? Before deciding, we made the following calculations:

Option 1, zero financing for 36 months $33,000 divided by 36 monthly payments of $916 per month. Total payments equal $33,000

Option 2, take $3000 rebate, put down $9000 and get a 6% loan--$33,000 minus the $3000 rebate, minus $9000 down payment equals $21,000 divided by 12 monthly payments of $1807 for 12 months. But with this option the cost of the interest totaled approximately $680 over the life of the loan.

So we opted to take the $3000 rebate and make higher payments over a shorter period of time saving $1420. Oh, by the way, since the loan is a home equity loan the interest may be tax deductible potentially generating some additional savings.

You can argue that I didn't add in the time value of money, or what my money could earn if I didn't put down so much as we did with option 2. But that's why I didn't add in the tax savings from the home equity loan. I figure it would be nearly a wash and paying off a loan and avoiding paying interest is guaranteed money. I'll take a guarantee anytime.

New Car Smell or the Sweet Smell of Saving

The point of this little exercise is not to suggest that taking a rebate is always a better option than taking zero percent financing. The point is to **do the math for yourself before deciding!** There are many loan amortization programs on free websites you can use to do the calculations. As mentioned our website, www.mymilitarymillionaire. com has the free tools to do these calculations. It took me about a minute to plug in the principal amount, term and interest rate. In this case a minute of time will save better than $1420.

So next time you're contemplating a car purchase, consider what you *need* in the car over what you **want**. Think about whether a late model used car will do just as well-- or at least good enough-- as compared to a new car. If you decide to buy a new car consider selling your old car yourself rather than trading it in to the dealer. See if you don't save the kind of money I've saved over the years taking this approach. The new car smell may be appealing to you, but I think you'll like the sweet smell of money in the bank even more.

Chapter Six

Thinking the Unthinkable

Then I heard the voice of the Lord saying,
"Whom shall I send, and who will go for us?"
And I said, "Here I am; send me!"

Isaiah 6

I honor our military service men and women who will go for us. It's not an easy calling. Military service is dangerous business. In peacetime-- which seems to have been too fleeting in my time-- training can be very dangerous and off duty lifestyles may be even more dangerous. When a Harrier pilot missed roll call at Marine Corps Command and Staff College, the Marine aviators would yell out "crashed and burned," with a macabre expression of gallows humor. The 82nd Airborne Division provides its troopers a safety holiday if there are no division fatalities in 82 consecutive days. During my decade in The Division, I saw precious few safety holidays. I've lost friends in support of the Global War on Terrorism. I've lost friends to training and non-combat operational accidents. One of my friends fought his way out of the jaws of death by surviving a sniper bullet to his lower torso. His determination to live played a crucial role in his surviving a wound that would have claimed the life of a less determined soldier. I'm pleased that he's still around to be a husband and dad to his family as well as selected by the Army to become a general. I'm honored to have Billy Don as a friend.

Sadly, not all live to tell about their brush with death. A sergeant who once drove for me died in a training accident while participating in Jump Master School. A fellow officer--who I was instrumental in assigning overseas--died shortly before his return in a helicopter accident. His wife is my friend and client. While attending Airborne school at Fort Benning, Georgia as an ROTC cadet, one of my classmates died during a physical training run. Ironically, a combat tested senior noncommissioned officer survived his dangerous tour of duty in Afghanistan only to lose his life when the tree that he was cutting down at his home fell on him. Also, too many service members lose their lives on the highway each year.

I've even had a couple of close calls—none particularly heroic though. On a maneuver range a bullet ricocheted close enough for me to hear it whistle by my ear. I was informed afterwards that if I could hear the bullet, it had already passed my head. The one you don't hear is the one that will get you. On another occasion, I was in the bed of a military transport that overturned. Vehicle accidents claim many military lives. As a lieutenant on a routine parachute operation, upon exit from the aircraft, I landed on another parachutist's canopy, preventing my canopy from properly inflating. I slid off the lower jumper's canopy and my main canopy inflated just an instant before I hit the ground with a decisive thud. I had not immediately activated my reserve when I saw my main canopy had not inflated because I did not want to risk an entanglement and injury to the jumper below me. A general, who was on the drop zone observing, had pulled his jeep up to me and asked, "Are you OK?" "Yes sir, I'm fine." I replied. The general then said, "I scratched the airborne operation due to weather (referring to the lightening and a heavy rain), why did you jump?" "Because sir, the green light came on inside the aircraft and the jumpmaster said "Go!", I replied. Then the general said, "Oh!" and drove off and left me to find my way in the dark and rain. God was especially good to me that night.

Injury and Death

After 20 years of serving commanders and soldiers I've learned that military rules often do not serve the individual. We have made some strides. Our great nation is more generous now with those who give their lives in military service for the country than just a few years ago. I'm proud to have been a part of the effort to change the public law to allow medical retirement for all service members who die on active duty. Under the old law, only those who were seriously injured or wounded-- "imminent" in medical speak and received a medical board--could be medically retired. The old law disadvantaged those who died without benefit of the medical board bureaucracy. I was present when a general officer contemplated filing a false casualty report, suggesting soldiers who perished in a helicopter crash, were still alive so the Army could conduct an imminent death retirement board. We were all heartbroken that a military family would not get the fullest possible death benefits because there was no time to conduct the board. With a heavy heart, the general finally agreed with me to report the truth. We should not put commanders in a position of even considering diverging from the truth to take care of a family. Changing the public law has helped considerably. This was not the only contentious casualty that involved me. One of the last cases that crossed my desk before I retired was that of former NFL football player and Army Ranger, Patrick Tillman.

I'm also proud to have provided a measure of comfort to the family of Sergeant Jamie Alford, who died in December, 2008. Jamie's case attained national attention when it was featured on *The O'Reilly Factor* in 2003. The story line that aired suggested that the Army had neglected Green Beret Sergeant Alford by medically retiring him after being diagnosed with Creutzfeldt-Jacob, a debilitating brain disease. It was conjectured that Jamie contracted the disease from consuming tainted food in Oman while on a military mission. His father, a retired Army Command Sergeant Major and his mother, a former soldier as well, gave a heart rending plea on *The O'Reilly Factor* for the Army to reinstate their son on active duty despite his fatal disease. The next morning after the airing on *The O'Reilly Factor*, I briefed the general officers of the Army Special Operations Command on what I could ascertain about the case overnight with the command Public Affairs Officer. Convinced that I knew the most about the case and the military medical retirement system, the Special Forces Commanding General, who did not know me by name said, "I want to send this kid out to meet the family with a battalion commander to make this right." I was charged with getting the family to reappear on the *O'Reilly Factor* with a positive story. It was no easy task, but certainly less difficult than the hell that Sergeant Alford and his family were going through.

Shortly after the meeting, I traveled out to Karnack, Texas with a Special Forces battalion commander, a flight surgeon and the Public Affairs Officer to meet the family. Before walking to the door of their modest country home, I told the group that we would be on the receiving end of the family's enmity toward the Army. I asked that we just let the Alford family vent—to have thick skin no matter what the family said. Admittedly, seeing this tough, battle tested Green Beret confined to a hospital bed in the den of his parent's home, kitten weak and semi-conscious broke out hearts. I wanted to weep, but needed to show restraint for the family's sake. I held Jamie's hand, closed my eyes and said a "Hail Mary" to myself for him. We then moved to the kitchen where we sat at the table with his parents and just listened. I felt the parents had some penned-up emotion to let out. When his parents were done talking, it was my turn. I explained that Jamie was medically retired, not as a punishment, but for his benefit, such as tax free medical retirement pay, free medical care and the like. I carefully outlined all the advantages of medical retirement. The family didn't care. They simply wanted Jamie to die with his boots on—on active duty. I told the family I would see what I could do to help. Afterwards, I called The Adjutant General of the Army, General Farisee, another outstanding leader, who was updating the Army leadership on the situation. She quickly agreed to the unusual request to let Sergeant Alford reenlist so he could die on active duty.

I share this heartrending story to show that *every* military casualty is unique, no matter the circumstances, even if they don't get the national media attention of *The O'Reilly Factor* or the Tillman case. Rest assured that if your family is touched by serious injury or death, there are systems in place to help you through an emotionally devastating time. From my experience, there are two separate and distinct facets that are common to all death cases: The emotional and the financial.

There are a variety of agencies established to help the family deal with a casualty. The first place to start is with your family support center and the chaplain. The obvious place for the survivor to turn is the unit. However, from my experience, the service member's unit can't always be relied upon to do everything the surviving spouse and family needs. For instance, a widow asked me to intervene on her behalf because the unit failed to return her husband's equipment and personal items. The unit didn't intend to be ignorant of the widow's feelings; they just wanted to keep the Green Beret's locker in the team room intact, as a memorial. On another occasion, the Casualty Assistance Officer (CAO) assigned to the family was interjecting her own personal and religious values into the situation that were not agreeable with the family. I was asked to replace the CAO and eventually built enough trust that the family asked me to perform the eulogy at the memorial service.

Financial Considerations

Among the potentially worst things a family can do is make long term financial decisions under the emotional distress associated with a casualty. I had a widow referred to me a year after her husband's death. She admittedly mismanaged the $250,000 Service Group Life Insurance (SGLI) payment with only about a third of the insurance payment remaining when she was referred to me. The benefit has since been raised to $400,000. It has taken us several years to improve her financial position. Another widow had been told to use her $250,000 SGLI benefit to pay off her mortgage when a better solution would have been a combination of paying off part of her mortgage and to take advantage of the tax benefits associated with home mortgage interest along with some conservative investing to generate current income, and purchasing term insurance since she still had minor aged children in the household. This Army widow is still my client and friend even though she has an immediate family member who is a financial professional. It's challenging enough to make sound financial decisions with a clear head. I can't imagine making those tough decisions while grieving the loss of a loved one.

So what counsel would I give to a new widow or widower? **It always depends on the individual situation and what is suitable for that family.** However, I believe it's generally best to put off major investment decisions for a year. I generally suggest maintaining some liquidity because it may be up to a year before the widow and children receive all their entitlements. Such was the case for Army widow Major Rebecca Eggers whose husband Dan was killed during combat actions in Afghanistan. Camp Eggers in Afghanistan stands in memorial to Dan. According to Rebecca, it took about a year before her family received all her benefits. Additionally, the Casualty Assistance Officer assigned to her case was well intentioned, but knew very little about what she should do to apply for all her military, Veteran's Administration and Social Security benefits. Additionally, for the first time, like many widows, she had to file her tax return as head of household. Much of this she had to figure out herself under the heavy burden of losing her husband and having to provide emotional support to her two children. From my experience, getting the family through the first anniversary of their loved one's death should precede most non-urgent investment decisions. For instance, it may take some time for the family to decide whether to stay in the current military community to maintain continuity for the children's schooling or move back home to be close to family for support.

Insurance

I believe that every service member should participate in Soldiers Group Life Insurance (SGLI). For a modest premium of about $28 per month, the beneficiary will receive a $400,000 death benefit. Your coverage is automatic unless you decline it. I urge you not to decline it. I prepare insurance policy applications for my clients who request them and I have yet to find a better insurance deal. Before you decide to decline the coverage, I would welcome a conversation about the benefit. Contact me through our website www.kennethheaney.com and let's talk about it. Some of SGLI's features are:

1. No refund for an unused death benefit
2. $400,000 maximum death benefit
3. Benefit may be paid in a lump sum or 36 monthly payments
4. Accelerated death benefit option of up to 50% for a terminally ill policy holder with less than 90 days to live.

When you retire from service SGLI terminates 120 days after leaving active duty, but may be replaced by Veterans Group Life Insurance (VGLI). For my military clients I do a comparison of VGLI and term insurance from the insurance carriers I work with to see which is advantageous for the client. In some cases the VGLI is a better deal but not always. For my own financial situation, I've found that multiple term insurance policies are less expensive than VGLI while meeting my insurance needs. You can find more detailed insurance information at www.mymilitarymillionaire.com.

A Word of Caution:

Use care when selecting the beneficiary for your SGLI. Check your beneficiary designation at least once a year, before deploying to a combat zone, or if your family situation changes. Over my 20 years in the service, I've seen too many times when families were terribly hurt when the insured service members did not keep their beneficiary information current. I've seen SGLI benefits denied to a current spouse and family and paid to a former spouse of a divorce who had been estranged from the service member for many years. I've seen benefits paid to the service members parents because the service member failed to update records to reflect spouses and children as beneficiaries. **There is no provision to change your beneficiary once you are deceased, so keep it up to date.**

Income Entitlements

The military is generous with benefits in the tragic event of the death of a service member on active duty. From my experience, the spouse and family can expect to receive ample income to carry on a modest lifestyle should a military spouse die on active duty. Your exact entitlement will be contingent upon rank, years of service and circumstances surrounding the death among other considerations. Here are some of the major entitlements in addition to SGLI that most next of kin can rely upon:

Free military housing or Basic Allowance for Housing for up to a year.

TRICARE health insurance and pharmacy coverage

A one-time Death Gratuity of $100,000

Dependency and Indemnity Compensation (DIC) or Survivor Benefit Plan (SBP) monthly payment of about $1500, plus $243 per minor child or $488 for a child incapable of self care.

The widow will have to select what combination of DIC and SBP which is most advantageous to that situation. The combination of DIC and SBP should make up the preponderance of the soldier's income.

Generally, I'd suggest putting death benefits assets in a FDIC insured savings account or a number of Certificates of Deposit with staggered maturity dates to obtain some income and maintain liquidity until the family establishes their survivor benefits and decides where it will reside. Further, if the deceased soldier participated in the Thrift Savings Plan, a Roth or Traditional IRA, an investment professional can help the surviving beneficiary obtain control of those assets. Typically, it will take a month to do so. Little can be done in gaining control of these assets until the beneficiary has a death certificate.

Additionally, there may be tax implications for survivors. There may be taxes due on retirement plan redemptions. Also, the children's benefits may be taxable. Survivors who are not tax savvy may need the assistance of a professional tax preparer. Again, maintaining some asset liquidity is especially important if there is a tax bill due that the family is not accustomed to paying. There may be tax avoidance or reduction strategies, such as converting an IRA to a Stretch IRA, or establishing Uniform Gift to Minor's Act or Uniform Trust for Minor's Act accounts for surviving minor children. The point is that most surviving families are not equipped to manage the intricacies of the tax code and will need some professional assistance. (Note: Stretch IRAs work best for investors who will not need the money in their IRA account during their lifetime for their own retirement needs. CDs are FDIC insured and offer a fixed rate of return, whereas both principal and yield of investment securities do have risk and may fluctuate with changes in market conditions.)

Rebecca Eggers explains, "I had a Business and Accounting degree when Dan died, and I still wasn't equipped to deal with these financial issues alone. There are so many good intentioned people out there who want to help, that really are not professionals and don't know what they're talking about. Sometimes, even the people the Army assigned to assist me didn't know what they were doing. I had to redo and resubmit forms. This resulted in a delay in my benefits and entitlements being paid. It took about a year before it was all straight. My advice is to find a professional you can trust. Find somebody who knows what they're talking about and does investments or taxes or works with the Social Security Administration routinely. Chances are the people you can trust for accurate advice may not be your family members or friends or even someone the military appoints to assist you."

Major Rebecca Eggers is doing fine. Since Dan's death she's managed to do an exceptional job at raising her two children and staying competitive in her military career. She's got a great future as an officer and a mom.

A Final Caution

I've been involved with death throughout my military and post military careers. Death brings out the best and worst in different people. I've seen military spouses provide compassion and care to surviving families beyond anything that could be expected. Unfortunately, I've also seen death bring out the worst in people. Friends and family may come out of the woodwork wanting money. As difficult as it is to believe, people in your life may see your tragedy as their opportunity to better their financial position. It happens all too frequently. An attorney who is one of my clients asked me to talk to a widow with about $600,000 in liquid assets and to serve as the Registered Representative for her investments because she felt she was not well served by her current investment advisor. I met with the woman and her attorney. I shared my analysis that she would be broke in about 6 years at the current rate of redemption of her investments. Despite living within her means, she was going broke because she had family members who were asking for tens of thousands of dollars at a time. I offered to provide her my services only if she would establish a trust to help preserve her investments and deny her family members' a means to pressure her for access to her assets. She did not have the heart to take my suggestion and tell her family she could no longer provide them with so much money. She did not become a client of mine. This is not a unique story. A friend of mine who lost her husband in combat told me that family members were pressuring her for money shortly after her husband was buried. You may need to find a way to be strong and say "no" to any friend or family member who comes to you looking for a handout.

Fortunately, military spouses and families are resilient by nature. The families I know who have been touched by death are all doing well. The best part of their lives is still ahead of them with many good things to come.

I serve those who have died in military service by providing careful, patient and empathetic financial consultation to their survivors who seek it. I provide consultation to widows of heroes who died as a private up to lieutenant colonel. I want to share with you some of the consultation I've have with the widows I serve. If you are a widow or know of a widow who may benefit from my counsel, I can be reached through our website at <u>www.mymillitarymillionaire.com</u>.

Chapter Seven

Investing

The rich man plans for tomorrow. The poor man plans for today.
Chinese Proverb

Nearly 30 years ago I purchased my first mutual fund shares as an investment. I opened the account with $300 received from my tax refund while a lieutenant. I had no clue what I was doing. I took the advice to invest in the mutual fund from a friend from high school and college who is a certified public account. By my standards the mutual fund has performed well and it's still in my portfolio to this day. It was dumb luck to have such a positive outcome, at least until I became wiser about mutual fund investing. The point is that we all should start investing sometime. The goal is that your investing outcomes will be positive without having to rely on blind faith like I did nearly 30 years ago. With this goal in mind-- to invest for success--***start early, think long term and seek professional advice.*** These tenets pertain to many types of investing you may want to undertake. The intent is to give you some food for thought to get started on your own investment plan.

Start Early and Think Outside the Can

I credit my parents with teaching me the value of saving for a rainy day. When I was a kid my dad soldered a lid with a slit in it onto a coffee can and made a bank for me that required a can opener to access the contents. My parents encouraged us kids to save for a family vacation to Disney World. I saved for months and the day before the vacation, my dad opened the can to reveal about $50 in savings that I could use anyway I wanted in the Magic Kingdom. It wasn't until years later that I learned that sometimes, in fact many times, there are better places for me to put my money than into a sealed coffee can. The essence of investing is thinking outside the can. The essence of thinking outside the can is starting early. I believe you are more likely to achieve your financial goals by investing a little bit early in life than trying to invest a lot later in life. Here's an example:

Let's say you want to retire from the military in 20 years and want to have $50,000 accumulated in savings. To accumulate $50,000 in 20 years of investing at a modest 5% rate of return you would have to invest $126 per month. Most of us could come up with $126 per month. However, if you wait 15 years to start investing, and want to accumulate that same $50,000 at a 5% rate of return you would have to invest more than $754 per month. If you think it's too hard to invest a little bit now, imagine how difficult it will be to save a lot later.

Let's take another approach to investing. Suppose you are in the grade of E-3, O-1 or WO-1. Based on the 2010 Department of Defense Basic Pay Table, let's assume you get promoted every 5 years and invest half your pay increases for promotion and longevity for 20 years at that same 5% return. Your investment would grow as follows*:

Grades	5th Year	10th Year	15th Year	20th Year
E3-E7	$8288	$36,239	$80,731	$161,055
O1-O5	$8288	$70,056	$190,398	$384,303

The hypothetical growth depicted serves as a powerful argument why it's important to invest early and habitually. The growth does not reflect taxation and is for illustrative purposes only. After 20 years of service, who would not want a six figure nest egg on top of military retirement? Wouldn't having that kind of portfolio make it easier to make postretirement decisions?

Investing early and making it part of a lifelong routine is so important that I encouraged my own son to start saving and investing at a very early age. By the time he was a toddler he appeared on national television putting change into his own can. This came about when I agreed to appear in a feature on *The Early Show* in 1997 about investing. For an entire day a camera crew followed my wife and I around to get background video footage for the television segment. Near the end of the day the producer interviewed us about our investments. The interview was broadcast weeks later. I found out about it when some of my soldiers told me they had seen me on *The Early Show* when they were watching during breakfast in the dining facility. I learned a couple of things from this experience. First, I'm not cut out for TV. I can't endure the hours of shooting video for the few minutes that actually gets aired. Secondly, I learned that I could not count on the media to get my message out to my military comrades: with a modest lifestyle, routine saving and investing and a little hard work one could have a successful military career and financial portfolio. When I finally saw a tape of the feature that aired I was disappointed that the focus was on my investment strategy and not on the military aspect as I would have liked. Third, I learned that the video taped interview was edited to make it appear we were being interviewed by a television personality when it was just an unknown producer asking the questions. I was pleased, however, that the producer used my idea to capture on tape my 4 year old son putting change into his bank—a metal can like the one I had when I was a kid. Today, my son is a teenager who is a relentless saver and investor. He has a savings account, checking account, two mutual funds and tracks several stocks daily. He's off to a good start with his financial future.

It's not too early for you or even your children to get started on their own investment journey.

*Note: Examples used as illustrations only. Actual results may vary. Rates used are hypothetical and cannot be used for investment advice.

Think Long Term

There's a reason why a car has a big windshield and a small rear view mirror—it's more important to look ahead to the future than focus on what's passed. Looking forward is just as important with investing. When I talk with prospective clients one of the first things I want to know is their view on their investment time horizon. If the prospect is thinking long term we can have a serious discussion about investing. If they do not--and many don't--I can't do much for them. I don't know how to invest for the short term. To me, investing for the short term is an oxymoron. I'm finding that it's difficult to get the very young, or what I call the "Twitterers" to think long term. The Twitterers are so conditioned to expect immediate gratification that they often don't want to consider waiting for something. It's not their fault. It's just the way we're raising our kids. Think about it. When I was a kid in the 1960's and 1970's we had to wait for everything. In the morning we had to wait for our sisters to use the one bathroom first before getting ready for school. How many Twitterers live in one bathroom houses now? We had to walk to school or to a corner bus stop and wait. Today the bus stops at the driveway for the "Twitterers." After school, we would turn on the television and wait a while for the tubes to warm up before the picture came on...not the "Twitterers." The Twitterers will challenge our ability to teach them some patience when it comes to investing as well as other important aspects of life.

Long term is a decade or more. That view is consistent with the Life Financial Events Time Line we discussed earlier where we thought about life events in 20 year increments. I consider 3 to 5 years mid-term. The Dow Jones Industrial Average (Dow) experienced a 20% return in the calendar year 2009, resulting in positive return for many of my clients. I had no way of knowing the Dow* would bounce back the way it did after sustaining deep losses in the 4th quarter of 2007 through the first quarter of 2009. Before the upswing began in March of 2009, the Dow was actually down for the better part of the 2000 decade. So if you want to increase your odds with a winning investment hand, think long term.

*Note: The Dow Jones Industrial Average is an unmanaged index that is generally considered representative of U.S. industrial stocks. The performance of an unmanaged index is not indicative of the performance of any particular investment. Individuals cannot invest directly in an index. Past performance is not a guarantee of future results. Actual results may vary.

Dictionary.com defines investing as, "to put (money) to use, by purchase or expenditure, in something offering potential profitable returns, as interest, income, or appreciation in value." I underscore "potential" because there are no guarantees that an investment will prove profitable. Also, the expenditure may be your time, your effort or you military entitlements in order to obtain a future profit or gain. I've been fortunate. In nearly 30 years of investing myself, I've never been forced to take a loss. During the past 30 years we've seen some years of excellent investment returns and years of terrible potential loss. I started investing in mutual funds in the 1980s not many years before one of the worst days in the stock market in my lifetime. That day, notoriously called "Black Monday," occurred on October 19th 1987. Our domestic stock markets and the world markets crashed that day. The Dow Jones Industrial Average dropped more than 500 points that day and closed at 1738. The Dow lost nearly 23 percent of its value in that one short day. Foreign markets, like those in the United Kingdom, Australia, Hong Kong and Spain dropped by an even greater percentage. There were reports of stock broker suicides in the media. As a relatively young investor, I shrugged off the bad market news of Black Monday, scrapped together all the spare change I could find, and invested even more in my mutual fund. My instincts were correct. The market rebounded and despite enduring the worst single day percentage drop in history, the Dow finished the 1987 year above where it started for a positive return. Intuitively I knew what Sir John Templeton, pioneer in global investing, meant when he said, "Bull-markets [or increasing markets] are born on pessimism, grow on skepticism, mature on optimism and die on euphoria."

More than 20 years after Black Monday I'm still following my instincts in down markets. In the beginning of 2009 I started funding my personal retirement plan way ahead of schedule because of the down market and my desire to take advantage of relatively lower market prices. Normally, I would have waited until April of 2010 to fully fund my retirement plan for tax year 2009, but because the market had been beat down so much by early 2009 I decided to fund my retirement plan ahead of my normal schedule. My return on investment proved to out pace the market recovery because of this strategy.

If you're new to investing or have never invested at all I hope to provide you some food for thought and a basis from which to start thinking about investing or maybe some new ideas about investing. **If you do invest, you could lose your principal.**

Investing can take many forms. Some invest in antique and classic cars. Some may invest in art. Others may trade stocks on a daily basis [known as *day traders*]. Still others invest in real estate. A few years ago I was participating in a seminar on government benefits when another participant told me he had 100% of his investments in property around Northern Virginia.* I asked him if he though it was risky not being diversified in other investments like bonds or mutual funds. He told me he felt safe because "Real estate always goes up. Sometimes it goes up a lot and sometimes it only goes up a little. But it always goes up." I asked him about the mid 1990s when the real estate market got soft in Northern Virginia. I had a professional associate who had to swallow a $50,000 loss to sell her home during that timeframe. He replied he didn't see anything like that happening in the foreseeable future. Only months after this seminar, the housing market started crumbling. I hope the individual who was so heavily invested in real estate wasn't hurt too badly.

The intent is to give you some ideas and concepts to think about in order to start investing. If you've followed closely, you're already reducing your spending habits and living well beneath your means and pay grade. You're enjoying inexpensive hobbies and cars. You're saving money. But what can you do with your savings other than the standard bank or credit union savings account?

*Note: No strategy can accurately predict market movements or guarantee a profit.

Investing in Our Nation

The first place I invested--even before I blindly purchased my first mutual fund shares--was with U.S. Savings Bonds. An easy and safe way to start investing is with *Series EE Savings Bonds*. It's easy because you can invest with a payroll allotment with an investment as little as $25. The government will even provide safekeeping for your bonds free of charge if you don't want the responsibility of safeguarding the actual bond. It's relatively safe because Savings Bonds are backed by the full faith and credit of the government. It's an investment because it is setting aside assets now for a future return of the principal and growth. Even better, Savings Bonds provide tax deferred interest. The interest rate varies over time. I started investing in Savings Bonds when I joined the Army in 1983. I still have the bonds today. Many of them may be redeemed tax-free if I use them for my son's qualifying college education expenses. It's disappointing that our government doesn't make a bigger effort to market Savings Bonds because I'd rather see Americans buying our nation's debt rather than foreign buyers like Japan, China and Russia.

Another reason I like Savings Bonds is because it helps to condition the investor to take a long view. For instance, the bonds cannot be redeemed for six months after purchase. If I want to redeem them for tax free interest, I have to use them for qualifying educational expenses for my son, thus further conditioning me to think long term. One of the down sides of bond investment is that the long term return is historically less than some other types of investments, such as mutual funds or stocks. However, should the stock market take another plunge like it did in 2008 or in October of 1987, having bonds with a safe and reliable positive return makes them even more attractive. And keep in mind that next to your service, it's still a patriotic thing to do. Do you think you may be interested in Savings Bonds and a payroll allotment? More information about Savings Bond investing can be found at <u>www. treasurydirect.gov</u>.

A 10% Annual Return...Guaranteed?

The Department of Defense Savings Deposit Program (SDP) provides members of the uniformed services serving in a designated combat zone the opportunity to safely build their savings. You can invest up to $10,000.00 may be earning 10% interest annually (compounded on a quarterly basis) and guaranteed by the government. Service members must be receiving Hostile Fire Pay and be deployed for at least 30 consecutive days, or 1-day in each of 3 consecutive months in order to participate in the program. If I could get a guaranteed 10% annualized return I'd take it as long as I could and I encourage my military clients to do the same. When you redeploy from the eligible combat zone you are then eligible to receive the proceeds and close out the SDP account. You can find out more about this program at the website: www.dfas.mil

Retirement Investing with the Thrift Savings Plan

The Thrift Savings Plan (TSP) has been available to civil servants for many years. On October 30, 2000, the Floyd D. Spence National Defense Authorization Act was signed; it extends participation in the TSP to members of the uniformed services, including the Ready Reserve. Shortly after the TSP became available to military members in 2001 I was asked by the then XVIII Airborne Corps Chief of Staff, General Stanley McChrystal, to do a presentation to the Corps General Staff. At the end of my short presentation I recommended that all military participate in the TSP. General McChrystal leaned forward in his chair at the head of the conference table that looked as long as the deck of an aircraft carrier and asked "Ken, what makes you an authority to make such a recommendation?" At that moment I wished my seat were at the other end of the deck and not next to General McChrystal. Holding up my USA TODAY Money page article with my photo on it I replied, "Sir, I don't believe I'm an authority, but these guys do." I added by joking, "And besides Sir, unlike you who lives in tax-payer subsidized housing (referring to his military quarters), I actually own my house." Fortunately for me General McChrystal had a sense of humor that day and laughed. In all seriousness, I cannot think of a better leader on active duty to win the war in Afghanistan then General McChrystal. He's an amazing officer.

One of the most convenient ways to invest for retirement is with the TSP. Much like a 401(K) plan in the private sector, you can set aside part of your income which may reduce your taxable income by investing pretax dollars. Reducing taxable income allows one to save on their taxes in a tax year. However, taxation will occur when you redeem the investment after age 59½. So one may be able to push taxation off into retirement years when income and taxation may be lower and participate in the potential for tax deferred growth. One of the downsides of the TSP is that there is no matching contribution from the government, so only you contribute to it. The TSP offers a variety of investment options from the relatively lower risk G Fund and F Fund to the higher risk C, S and I Funds. It also offers target date maturity funds such as the various L Funds. So the TSP offers a variety of investment options to match your risk tolerance and time horizon. Nearly all of my military clients participate in the Thrift Savings Plan at my suggestion. All are surprised when I recommend they do so because there is no commission benefit for me to make such a recommendation. I tell them that my goal is to aid them in obtaining the best financial position available, regardless of any benefit to me. I know my investment practice will not only thrive, but flourish so long as the investment strategies I recommend are in the client's best interest, not mine.

You can find out more about the *Thrift Savings Plan* on the web at www.TSP.org. However, there are times when I suggest my military clients consider not investing with the *Thrift Savings Plan*. The following information comes directly from this website:

What are the major features of the TSP?

You may elect to contribute any percentage of your basic pay. However, your annual dollar total cannot exceed the Internal Revenue Code limit, which is $16,500. If you contribute to the TSP from your basic pay, you may also contribute from one to 100 percent of any incentive pay or special pay (including bonus pay) you receive, up to the limits established by the Internal Revenue Code.

The TSP website, www.TSP.org, offers the following information and more:

- Before-tax savings and tax-deferred investment earnings
- Low administrative and investment expenses
- A choice of investment funds:
    - Government Securities Investment (G) Fund
    - Fixed Income Index Investment (F) Fund
    - Common Stock Index Investment (C) Fund
    - Small Capitalization Stock Index Investment (S) Fund
    - International Stock Index Investment (I) Fund
    - Lifecycle (L) Funds
- Catch-up contributions for participants age 50 or older
- In-service withdrawals for financial hardship or after you reach age 59½
- Portable benefits and a choice of withdrawal options after you separate from service
- Ability to designate beneficiaries for your account balance
- Spouses' rights protection for loans and withdrawals and recognition of qualifying court orders
- An automated telephone service (the ThriftLine) for account information and certain transactions

What if I can't afford to contribute very much?

You can contribute as little as one percent of your basic pay each pay period. Even small savings add up over time. If you put in only $40 from your pay each month, here's the approximate amount you could have in your TSP account in 20 years.

$40 monthly contributions	$9,600
Earnings (assuming 7% a year)	11,359
Your total in 20 years*	**$ 20,959**

In addition to your savings with the TSP, you will be reducing your taxable income creating more savings.
*Note: Example used as illustration only. Actual results may vary. Rates used are hypothetical and cannot be used for investment advice.

When to Say No to the TSP?

When do I suggest my military clients not invest retirement assets with the TSP? When during the time my client is deployed to a tax exempt combat zone we consider the Roth IRA and mutual funds. The reason is simple. If my client is not paying income taxes because he or she is deployed to a tax exempt combat zone, then the tax benefit from investing with the TSP may be eliminated or negligible. If there is no taxable income, there can be no deferred taxation by investing in the Thrift Savings Plan. In this case a Roth IRA and mutual funds may make more sense. A Roth IRA allows assets to potentially grow tax free, but there is no immediate reduction of taxable income as with the Thrift Savings Plan.

I attended a promotion ceremony reception in Washington DC when a general who I had served with years earlier asked me for some financial insight. He said his son, an Army Lieutenant, was getting ready to invest about $10,000 in the Thrift Savings Plan before he deployed to Iraq. He asked if this was a sound investment strategy. I said, "Sure it is. It's a fine strategy, but it doesn't optimize your son's tax position." "How's that," the general asked. I explained that with his proposed strategy his son would potentially obtain tax deferred growth for his investment. However, he would likely receive no immediate tax benefit because he would have little or no income tax due while deployed to the tax exempt combat zone of Iraq. I said that if he put his investment into a mutual fund under the provisions of the Roth IRA, his potential growth would be tax free. Tax free is normally a better strategy than tax deferred in this situation. The general replied "Thanks Ken. I guess that's why you're an investment professional and I'm not" with a smile. If you want more information about establishing a Roth IRA for yourself, contact me at www.mymilitarymillionaire.com and I will help you get started. There, under the "Leaning Center" tab, you can find all sorts of tax information including The Armed Forces' Tax Guide.*

*Note: To qualify for the tax free penalty free withdrawal of earnings, a Roth IRA must be in place for at least five tax years, and the distribution must take place after age 591/2 or due to death, disability, or a first time home purchase (up to $10,000 lifetime maximum). Before taking any specific action, be sure to consult with your tax professional.

When is a House More Than a Home?

A house is more than a home when it's an investment. So many military families leave assets on the sidelines because they choose to rent or live in government housing rather than own their home. However, if you are willing to consider buying a home and take risk, there is potential for financial gain. Even though I've been an investor in the stock market for more than 25 years, much of my wealth has come from real estate purchase, ownership and sale. While serving on active duty I managed to accumulate about a $250,000 return on investment through real estate.

As we've seen with the meltdown of the real estate market in the last five years, it's possible to lose money. However, if you are military, you have advantages in the real estate market that others may not have, making a home purchase worthy of serious consideration. What are those advantages?

First, there is the housing allowance that is available in most locations. That housing allowance can range from hundreds to thousands of dollars per month.

Second, the housing allowance is tax free. If you were working in the commercial sector you can bet that if you received a housing allowance you would likely be taxed on it. So the tax free provision of the military housing allowance is particularly generous.

Third, there are provisions in the tax code that provide the military relief from taxation associated with a home sale if the sale if related to a permanent change of station move.

Beyond these advantages there are several ways to profit from home ownership such as:

First, the property can increase in value.

Second, there may be tax benefits such as deductions for mortgage interest, closing costs or other tax incentives.

Third, the property can be rented for income.

Fourth, the property can be sold for profit.

Also, there is more flexibility in home ownership than meets the eye. If a new assignment takes you to a different location you can sell the home or rent it if you feel like you'll return in the future. Most military installations have a housing office that will facilitate the advertising to other service members the sale or rental of your home.

If you want some additional income, you can sublet your home. You can rent part of your house. I own a home near Fort Bragg, North Carolina that I have sublet for five years. The house is divided into the main house with a separate guest quarters. The guest quarters has a laundry room, galley kitchen and six other rooms, a separate driveway and entrance. We originally intended this area for guests. But we've been able to lease part of the house for about three quarters of the mortgage, insurance and taxes for the home. The home also has 4 acres of fenced horse pasture and a barn. Since we no longer have horses at the property, we lease the pastures and the barn as well. The ability to sublet is not just an option for large homes with land. A couple of decades ago when I bought my first home, I took on a roommate to help with the house payment. Also, when I was sent off to Florida for about five months of training, I found short term tenants to lease the house while I was gone. As you can see, there are many options with leasing that may help you with the affordability of your home.

Obviously, buying a home is a serious matter and should never be entered into without careful consideration. I believe that with the housing market decline of a few years ago, there are many great buying opportunities. Before buying a property, you will want to obtain the assistance of a realtor who will work for you and protect your interests. A good place to find a realtor is through a trusted friend's referral. Not all our experiences with realtors have been spectacular. In fact, one ignorant realtor who helped us buy a home in Maryland quit returning our calls after the sale was complete. In another instance, our realtor posted a picture of the wrong home when advertising our home for sale in the multi-listing. Notwithstanding, most of our experiences with realtors have been positive and very helpful. Look for a realtor who takes the time to get to know you, your needs and budget. Never let a realtor pressure you into a sale. Many years ago, there was a $500 difference between what we wanted to pay for a home and how much the seller wanted. I suggested the realtor make up the difference in his commission. This short sighted realtor called me and using profanity explained how I don't get to negotiate with his commission which would have been around $8000. We walked away from the house and found a much nicer house for the price we wanted to pay. We still own the house today. Much like with buying a car, in the real estate market the deal of the century comes around about once a week! So, if one of your dreams is to own a home, and you have the means to do so, why wait when there are many incentives available right now?

Education

"Mom always said, 'Get an education.' Well mom, now I'm a graduate of the University of Fort Bragg, School of the 82ND Airborne Division."
CSM (Ret.) Polito Robles at his retirement ceremony.

Like my friend Polito Robles, I received much of my education at Fort Bragg both metaphorically and literally. Five years after graduating from the University of Delaware, I obtained my first of two master's degrees at Webster University at Pope Air Force Base, adjacent to Fort Bragg. The tuition assistance paid for half of the tuition cost—a great deal at the time. Later the Army sent me to obtain a second masters degree which was fully funded—an even better deal. Also, my wife obtained her bachelors and master's degrees with the help of the Fort Bragg and Deatrick Education Offices.

Too many service members do not take advantage of their military educational benefits and leave a great investment untapped. The common excuse is "I don't have time." I know that is an excuse you will not repeat because reading this book is a great first step in what should be a lifetime of education. With online courses, access to civilian education could not be easier or more convenient. Back in the mid 1980s when I got my first advanced degree, many commanders believed in the importance of civilian education, but they did not want their subordinates distracted by the rigors of going to school. I received skeptical approval to go to night school on my own time:

The benefits are well worth the effort and are more than just personal enrichment. There are tangible benefits to continuing your education. According to a study cited by Educationatlas.com:

Adults ages 25 to 65 who worked at any point throughout duration of the study period received average annual earnings of $35,000. Average earnings varied in amount by level of education; $18,900 for high school dropouts, $25,900 for high school graduates, $45,400 for college graduates, and $99,300 for persons possessing a professional degree (J.D, M.D., D.V.M., or D.D.S). Evidence suggests that each consecutive higher education level a person receives is directly related to increase in earnings.

You may believe that because you are military, your income is determined by the military pay tables alone. However, all of the services agree that both military and civilian education are key elements of advancement and job assignments. Today, incentives and benefits for continuing your education are the best since World War II. The Post 9/11 GI Bill is very generous and provides assistance with tuition, books, housing and may even be transferable to eligible family members. You can find your exact benefits at www.gibill.va.gov. I suggest you make an appointment today with your installation's education office to talk to a counselor about your benefits.

Whether it's investing in the Thrift Savings Plan, Savings Bonds, the Savings Deposit Program, or taking advantage of your housing allowance or educational benefits, the military offers many ways for you to easily and conveniently do as the rich person does and plan for tomorrow by investing today!

Conclusion

Your Financial Future

If you don't know where you are going, you might wind up
someplace else.

Yogi Berra—Baseball Great

I wish I had had a crystal ball 30 years ago to see where I would
be today. I would not have worried nearly as much. Financially, I
would have done things pretty much the same, but I would have not
been so concerned about whether I was on the right track. I would
have worried less about my public school education, my military
career, my son's upbringing or my second career. I'm in a pretty
comfortable place in life because I thought about the future and
did the best I could to shape it despite the curve balls that life can
throw. You don't have a crystal ball either. **However, I believe your
financial future can be brighter. Set your goals and track them
with a timeline. Take advantage of your military benefits. Live
beneath your means. Make saving a habit. Keep hobbies and
cars inexpensive. Avoid bad debt. Invest part of your income and
raises and keep your family involved. Above all *stay military*!**

By the Numbers

Before parting, here is my best shot at giving you a hypothetical
look into the future if you stay military in current dollars:

--Enlisted active duty pay average for 20 years, $772,000; (Source: www.dfas.mil)

--Housing allowance, $108,000 (Assuming 15 years at avg. rate of $600/month average); (Source: www.dfas.mil)

--Federal tax incentives, $72,000; (Source: www.irs.gov)

--Education benefits, $35,000; (Source: www.va.gov)

--Health care benefit after retirement, $311,000 (Source: Prudential Insurance Company);

--Thrift Savings Plan; $66,000 (Assuming $2000 per year average investment at 5% annual growth)

--Other savings and investments, $150,000;

--Retirement pay for 35 years, $936,000;

--Total: $2,450,000

(These calculations are hypothetical for illustrative purposes and your circumstances may be different.) I'd bet that when you took your oath of enlistment or office you had any idea a military career could be worth so much!

How Do You Measure Success?

Driving with my son Josh to his band rehearsal I notice we are following a sports car with a Fort Myer vanity license plate that proclaims "Two Star." Josh notices the plate and asks, "Dad, do you ever wish you stayed in the Army longer? Maybe you could have made general yourself." I reply, "Josh, I don't think about that much. I don't spend much time looking in the rear view mirror. There's a reason, son, why the windshield of the car is big and the rear view mirror is small. We should be looking forward." Then he asks, "In your own judgment, are you a success? I mean you have the respect of a lot of people and we're the most well off family I know. But do you feel like a success?" I glance over at him with a smile and respond, "Josh, it's too early to tell. We've done well financially, sure, but I can't say I'm a success until you're on your own pursuing a career, with your own family and a productive member of the community. When you do those things, I'll consider myself a success. Just like when I was in the Army, I measured my success by the accomplishments of those who served under and with me. The same applies with my service as an investment professional; my clients must be successful for me to succeed. The goal is to give back more than you take."

Is there an investment lifestyle topic you would like me to speak about at your event? Let me know by contacting me at <u>www. mymillitarymillionaire.com</u>.

"War is an ugly thing, but not the ugliest of things. A man who has nothing which he is willing to fight for...is a miserable creature who has no chance of being free, unless made and kept by the exertions of better men than himself."--John Stuart Mill

Thank you and your family for your exertions to keep us free!

About the Author

Although Ken Heaney is new to book authorship he is no stranger to the military or investing. Ken served more than 20 years in the Army primarily at Fort Bragg, North Carolina in the 82D Airborne Division and the U.S. Army Special Operations Command. His military service has taken him to Asia and the Middle East in peace and war. Ken's investment experience spans nearly 30 years and has been featured by *USA Today*, *Kiplinger Personal Finance* and *The Early Show*. Ken is currently a partner at an investment services practice where he provides thoughtful, patient and carefully researched investment, retirement and tax reduction strategies for individual clients and corporations. He provides lively presentations for military, government, business and charitable events on economic and personal financial issues and can be reached at www.kennethheaney.com or www.mymilitarymillionaire.com for speaking engagements. Ken spends his free time between his farms near Southern Pines, North Carolina and Gettysburg, Pennsylvania.

Notes

Opinions voiced in this book are not intended to provide specific advice and should not be construed as recommendations for any individual. To determine which investment products and strategies may be appropriate for you, consult with your financial, tax or legal professional. Please remember that investment decisions should be based on your individual goals, time horizon, and tolerance for risk.

All charts and diagrams are hypothetical. Your results may vary

Securities offered through National Planning Corporation (NPC), Member FINRA/SIPC. Brown & Associates and NPC are separate and unrelated companies.